JOURNEYING
WITH THE SPIRIT

JOURNEYING
WITH THE SPIRIT

Jacqueline McMakin
and
Rhoda Nary

HarperSanFrancisco
A Division of HarperCollinsPublishers

FIRST EDITION

Library of Congress Cataloging-in-Publication Data
McMakin, Jacqueline.
    [Doorways to Christian growth]
    The doorways series / Jacqueline McMakin and Rhoda Nary.—1st ed.
      p. cm.
    Originally published as a single volume in 1984, under the title:
Doorways to Christian growth.
    Includes bibliographical references.
    Contents: [1] Encountering God in the Old Testament—[2] Meeting
Jesus in the New Testament—[3] Journeying with the spirit—[4]
Discovering your gifts, vision, and call.
    ISBN 0–06–065377–9 (v. 1).—ISBN 0–06–065378–7 (v. 2).—ISBN
0–06–065379–5 (v. 3).—ISBN 0–06–065380–9 (v. 4).
    1. Christian life—1960- 2. God—Biblical teaching. 3. Jesus
Christ—Person and offices. I. Nary, Rhoda. II. Title.
[BV4501.2.M4358 1993]
248.4—dc20   92–53917
                                               CIP

93 94 95 96 97 ❖ RRD(H) 10 9 8 7 6 5 4 3 2 1

This book is printed on acid-free paper that meets the American National Standards Institute Z39.48 Standard.

CONTENTS

INTRODUCTION

In a few crowded offices in Hyattsville, Maryland, a handful of people working for peace and justice have formed the Quixote Center. Believing that all peoples on Earth are cherished by God, they remind us of the corollary, that each of us is called to embody that love. Here is how they describe themselves:

A gathering of people
who will work and pray
with laughter,
to reach for stars that seem
too distant to be touched, or
too dim to be worth the effort.
We will try to be friends
with persons in need,
and to celebrate life with people who believe
that the struggle to follow Jesus in building
a world more justly loving,
is worth the gifts of their lives.[1]

What a beautiful way to describe what it means to follow Jesus. Quixote Center member William Callahan, in his book *Noisy Contemplations*, elaborates:

Our call is to follow Jesus, not as slavish imitators of his actions but as people who re-express his spirit in our day. Our guide to this 'balanced' way of living is the great commandment. We must love God, love ourselves and love our neighbors near and distant with a love that shows forth in our decisions and deeds.[2]

If we say "yes" to the call to follow Jesus, we open the door to continual growth and challenge. How to nurture that growth is the purpose of this volume. Centered around the question "How can I nourish my spirit?," this book offers tools from the treasure of Christian experience, tools that we, too, have found vital in our lives.

The first two *Doorways* books introduced some of the many tools for growth in the tradition: Bible reflection, prayer, caring for one another, commitment. In this third book we deal with these tools more thoroughly and offer some additional ones. The challenge is to move beyond tasting to incorporating some of these practices more permanently into our lives.

The assumption in this book and *Discovering Your Gifts, Vision, and Call* is that joining together in some kind of communal effort is an important aspect of Spirit living. This third book, when used as a course, offers training in some of the inward practices that enable community to develop.

Each session in this volume offers a particular tool for growth and a specific type of prayer. The first session, "Saying 'Yes' and Saying 'No,'" focuses on commitment and invites us to express that in a *prayer of consecration*.

The second session, "Listening," explores listening to God, ourselves, and others and introduces *listening prayer*.

In the third session, "Recalling Our Stories," we look back over our lives and reflect on God's presence along the way. This process is undergirded with prayer for others, called *intercession*.

Reliving our story may reveal the need for inner healing. This is the subject of the fourth session, "Cleansing and Healing." The prayer known as *healing of memories* is introduced here.

In Session 5, "Living with a Generous Spirit," we ask what changes related to time, money, energy, work, and other life choices would liberate us to express God's love more fully. For help with these choices we focus on the *prayer of discernment*.

Finally, in Session 6, "Food for the Journey," we consider the particular types of spiritual nourishment we want to incorporate into our lives.

In this book we highlight these resources from the Christian tradition to address our own God-hunger. Strengthened by them, we can then be agents of reconciliation and liberation in the estranged and oppressed places to which God calls us.

PREFACE TO
THE DOORWAYS SERIES

Two of us were rambling along a trail on a sparkling spring day. One was discouraged, did not know where her life was going. The other felt content and grateful for time to see what was happening in the woods.

Suddenly we stopped. Across our path lay a branch, broken off and seemingly dead. But there right on that branch burst forth a blossom that beamed at us in greeting.

We looked at each other and smiled. In that flower, God had broken in on us with a message: life can burst forth unexpectedly and bless us with its presence.

This brief story came to mind as we were thinking about the purpose of the four books in the *Doorways* Series. They are for people with hope, energy, and commitment who want reinforcement. They also are for dispirited people who question the direction of their own lives and of society.

The books invite you to taste nourishing spiritual food discovered by people in one particular faith path—the Christian tradition. From the core of this tradition radiates an astounding truth: there is at the heart of the universe a cherishing presence that holds all creation in a loving embrace. To be nurtured by this (love) is to be infused by fresh life.

In a fast-moving, multifaceted society, people look for anchors to hold them steady. Mobility makes us long for a sense of belonging. Pressing personal and societal needs make us wonder where we fit and how we can contribute.

The *Doorways* Series was written in response to these yearning. It helps us listen to our own truth and sink our roots in a solid tradition. It takes us on a journey of discovery. Its purpose is to help us grow in spiritual awareness, learn to build community where we are, and be more fully God's person at home, at work, and in the other places where we spend our time.

Underneath our yearnings are profound questions. Each book in the *Doorways* Series focuses on one question most of us ask at one time or another:

✤ Who is God?

✤ Who is Jesus?

✤ How can I nourish my spirit?

✤ What should I do with my life?

To aid you in addressing these questions, this series offers twenty-four dynamic stories, images, and concepts found in the Christian tradition. When you allow all parts of your body, mind, and spirit to engage with these treasures, you will be enlarged, enhanced, empowered.

Included in each book are activities for you, the reader, as well as for a group. Thus, each book can be used as a course. Designed originally by a community of Catholic and Protestant laypeople, the courses include wisdom and practices from each tradition that we have found powerful in our own lives. The courses build on each other, but each can be used on its own.

In their time with Jesus, the disciples had a training experience—living, learning, doing. They moved from being neophytes to well-trained healers and teachers. These courses are designed to replicate this experience of growth for us twentieth-century people, to equip us to live the committed life. Each of the *Doorways* courses presents a different challenge.

Encountering God in the Old Testament provides a way to explore the understandings of God realized by people in the Old Testament. This introductory course is suited to people with no prior experience of faith as well as to longtime churchgoers who are taking another look at the meaning of faith.

Meeting Jesus in the New Testament offers opportunities to learn about the Jesus of history and to make faith decisions today in response to the living presence of the Spirit. It is for those who want to be more than observers of the ministry of Jesus, who want to explore being companions in that work.

Journeying with the Spirit is for those who are committed to the way of Jesus and who would like to strengthen that commitment through experiencing classic resources for growth such as prayer, meditation, healing, and reconciliation.

Discovering Your Gifts, Vision, and Call is for people concerned with the pain and disharmony in the world and who want to help implement God's vision for the world. It offers a discernment process for discovering one's gifts and calling as well as ideas for forming communities to give communal expression to it.

These four courses are progressive in that they build on a deepening relationship with God and provide opportunities to:

✦ *explore* experiences of God;

✦ *decide* about one's relationship to God;

✦ *deepen* those decisions;

✦ *discern* life direction and purpose.

We offer these books to each of you as you seek to find your particular way of making the world a better place. If current environmental degradation teaches anything, it is that every person on Earth must become involved in preserving this precious creation. To build the kind of global resolve necessary will require commitment and stamina, which come from being firmly rooted in sources of spiritual power.

HOW TO USE THIS BOOK
AS A COURSE

This book is designed not only to be read but to be used as a course for individuals and groups. As an individual, you can gain much from "doing" this book in your own way and in your own timing. Adapt the Group Design exercises to yourself and try them out. Do the Individual Work. Perhaps you can find another person with whom to share the course or to discuss some of its aspects. If you are motivated to work alone with the content, honor that instinct and have confidence that your efforts will bear fruit.

Groups that can benefit from the material are existing Bible-study, life-sharing, or task groups who want to grow together, or groups especially convened for the particular training offered through these courses.

✤ How the Material Is Organized ✤

Each book includes an introduction, six sessions, and ideas for further reflection and next steps. Each of the six sessions includes:

✤ Session Text: basic content material on the topic;

✤ Group Design: practical ways for a group to work with the content in the session text;

✤ Individual Work: suggestions on how to apply the content to our own lives as individuals.

✤ Using the Material in Groups ✤

In order to get the most from the course, it is important to do three things:

1. Read and Digest the Text. Before coming to the first meeting, read the introduction, How to Use This Book as a Course, and the Session 1 text in preparation. To prepare for the second session, read the text for Session 2, and so on through the six sessions of the book. It is best to devote most of your time between meetings to the Individual Work related to the preceding session before reading the new session. Leave the new session for the day or so before you meet.

2. Participate in the Group Design. When people relax and participate in the group activities, much growth occurs. No design is perfect, and no design works equally well for all groups. Don't be bound by these design ideas, but do take time to understand their underlying purpose. If you can accomplish the same goals in other ways, great. You may want to modify the timing on the designs. We estimate that our timing works easily for groups of about twelve people. Smaller groups will have more time; larger groups may have to shorten or omit certain activities.

Each Group Design has several parts that we will look at in detail.

Gathering Time: The purpose of this is to assemble the group and ready yourselves for the session. Since we have built in ways to share personal information throughout the design, this does not have to be accomplished fully in the gathering time. Ten minutes is usually sufficient. Divide the time equally among all of you and really listen to each person. Resist the temptation to allow more time for this section or to be undisciplined in its use.

Sharing Groups: These are groups of four that you form at the first session. The purpose of these is to share in a small setting what you did with the suggestions for the Individual Work and to support one another as you take the course. These same groups meet at least once during each session. We find there are many benefits when the same group meets consistently. To get to know others in the larger group, there are activities to do with them in other parts of the session.

Discussion of the Session Text: We have included discussion of the text only occasionally because we felt it useful to give more time to other activities. However, if your group would like to discuss it each time, feel free to do so. Here's a sample discussion question: What learning from the text was most important for you?

Lab Exercise: The purpose of the lab exercise is to enable the group to experience one aspect of the topic and reflect on this experience. The activities in this section vary a great deal. Some are lighthearted, while others are more serious. Participants have found them all to be valuable.

Closing: This time is meant to give people an opportunity to reflect on the session and to have closure. Sometimes we offer a suggestion about how to do this; at other times we leave it to you. Some groups like to vary their closing exercises; others like the consistency of the same ending each time, such as a favorite song or a circle of prayer.

Materials: We suggest that you bring a Bible and a notebook for each session. When additional materials are needed, this is indicated in the design.

Breaks: According to your group's needs, schedule a five- to ten-minute break in the middle of each session. Our estimated timing does not include breaks, so adjust your timing accordingly. Tell people at the beginning of the session when the break will be.

3. Do the Individual Work. This work is designed to be done at home between sessions and is an important part of the course. It is a bridge between sessions and provides ways for you to integrate the material. Our participants find this one of the most worthwhile parts of the experience and urge us to underscore it.

The Individual Work usually involves fifteen to thirty minutes of quiet time per day for reading, reflection, and writing your thoughts in a journal, usually a loose-leaf notebook. At the end of each week it is useful to write a one-paragraph summary of what you did, your particular learnings and difficulties, and any questions. This summary can be shared with the group.

We suggest that you devote the quiet times during the first part of your week to the Individual Work and use the last few days before your group session to read the new chapter in preparation for the next session.

For the six weeks of the course, budget the time you need to do the Individual Work. It is integral to the course.

✤ What About Leadership? ✤

Don't rely on just one person to make your group thrive. Leadership is needed for two functions: *facilitation* and *organization*. Consider finding two people for each function. Choose these people on the basis of gifts and motivation. Who would really like to do what?

Facilitation: This can be done by the same person or pair each time or rotated so everyone in the group takes a turn. As the group facilitator you will:

✤ read the session text, Group Design, and Individual Work in advance;

✤ gather the necessary materials for the next session;

✤ convene the group at the start of the session;

✤ lead it through the Group Design, keeping to the time you agree on;

✤ close the meeting with a reminder of the time and place of the next session.

There are additional ways you as a facilitator can help the group. You might:

✤ do some background reading.

✤ add your creativity to the Group Design, tailoring it to the needs of the group.

✤ pray for the people in the group.

✤ give examples from your own life to begin sharing times. The way you do this modeling is important. If your example is long, other people's examples will be long. If you share from the heart, others are likely to do the same. By your example you give others freedom to be open. Our participants tell us that when they hear leaders share authentic pains and joys, they feel encouraged to face similar feelings in their own situations.

✤ be attentive to nonverbal communication in the group. As a leader, you can foster an atmosphere of caring, genuineness, and openness through a smile, a word of encouragement, a touch on the arm.

Organization: This, too, can be done by the same person or pair each time, or rotated. To help in this way you can:

✤ publicize the course by placing notices in newsletters, making personal phone calls to invite people to attend, and distributing flyers;

✤ be attentive during the session to people's reactions and lend encouragement to those who need it;

✤ call absent people between times to fill them in on what happened;

✤ see that refreshments are provided, if the group wishes them;

✤ pray for the individuals in the group.

We call the organization people *shepherds* since they look after and care for each person individually, leaving the facilitators free to care about group process and content. After facilitating courses with the assistance of shepherds, we would never be without them. They make a major difference in the quality and depth of a course. Shepherding is a wonderful gift that some people have and enjoy using.

✤ How to Gather a Group ✤

Suppose you would like to gather a group to take a *Doorways* course together. Find another person who will work with you and who has enthusiasm about doing the course. Consider whether to seek church sponsorship. To find people who would like to take the course and to prepare them to participate fully, you can do these things:

1. *Spread the word as widely as possible.*

Start with family, friends, neighbors, members of groups active in the church and community, and newcomers. Try to contact these people personally. Tell them the purposes of the course: to provide spiritual nourishment, to build a caring and supportive group, to discover which part of God's work we are called to foster. (To become clearer about the purpose for each course, read the introductory material in the beginning of the course.)

People respond to an invitation to join the course for a variety of reasons: some are looking for a sense of belonging; others want purpose or direction in their lives; others are hungry for spiritual nourishment. Find out what people are looking for and then describe how the course addresses that need.

2. *Be sure to go over procedural matters such as the dates, time, and place for the course.*

If possible, hold the course in a comfortably home-like atmosphere.

Explain that the course depends on the commitment of all the members to come regularly, to be on time, to do the Individual Work, and to let someone know if they will be absent so they can be brought up-to-date before the next session.

3. *Let people know that the method used will be experiential learning.*

This style depends on the participation of each person and not on the expertise of a leader. Participants learn by doing. You each proceed at your own pace and in your own way. Some people will have important insights during the group meetings; others may have them at home; others may see results from the course only after it has ended.

This style of learning contrasts with traditional ways of teaching in which someone in authority (a theologian, pastor, or teacher) offers content to a learner, whose main job is to assimilate and apply it. Some people may expect a traditional approach and ask questions such as "Who's teaching the course? Who's the leader?" Sometimes we offer this explanation: The traditional approach is useful for imparting doctrine (the wisdom and teachings of the church throughout history). Experiential learning enables us to examine some of those doctrines and make them a living part of our lives. The facilitators of the course are learners with all the others who take it.

4. *Pray together for the group.*

That can make the difference between gratitude and frustration in gathering a group. When you pray, you may be given inspiration about new people to contact or new ways to do it.

5. *Determine the size and makeup of the group.*

The course works well with groups numbering from ten to twenty, people of all ages, clergy and laity, men and women.

SESSION 1

Saying "Yes" and Saying "No"

If you had the task of describing what God is like, and you wanted to do it in a way everyone could understand, how would you do it?

Faced with this challenge, Jesus told the story of a runaway boy who squandered his resources, lived a wild life, and finally decided to return home. How did the father react? With anger, disdain, indifference? No. According to Luke, the father's response was completely unexpected:

> He ran to the boy, clasped him in his arms and kissed him tenderly. (Luke 15:21, JB)

God is like the father in this unlikely tale. According to Jesus, God runs to meet us and wraps us in an embrace. To help us consider and respond to this amazing reality is the purpose of this session.

Even if we are unable to recognize God's care or have turned from it, according to Jesus God's love remains constant, ready to flow toward us whenever we are able to accept it. In Jesus' story, the father has no need for an apology from his wayward child. So great is his joy at the son's return, he only wants to celebrate! Calling for the best clothes, the finest food, music, and dancing, he throws a big party to mark the boy's return.

Like the boy, no matter what our condition, we are invited to return God's embrace and join in celebration. Jesuit paleontologist Pierre Teilhard de Chardin is one who responded wholeheartedly to this invitation:

What can I do to gather up and answer that universal and enveloping embrace? . . . To the total offer that is made me, I can only answer by a total acceptance. I shall therefore react . . . *with the entire effort of my life*—of my life of today and of my life of tomorrow, of my personal life and of my life as linked to all other lives.[1]

As with most of us, the "entire effort" of Teilhard's life was marked by what he called times of development and diminishment. Throughout his life, he developed his scientific investigations into the origin of the human species, and considered them to be expressions of the creative power of God. The inner motivation for his work he described this way: "I merge myself, in a sense, through my heart, with the very heart of God."[2]

These periods of development, he realized, are interspersed and finally replaced with times of diminishment. When we are unable to work, or are diminished by ill health, old age, rejection, or failure, then it is, thought Teilhard, that we can be born more fully into God's love. Related to those moments, Teilhard prayed:

> . . . in all those dark moments, O God, grant that I may understand that it is You (provided only my faith is strong enough) who are painfully parting the fibres of my being in order to penetrate to the very marrow of my substance and bear me away within Yourself.[3]

Teilhard's response to God's embrace was full and wholehearted in good times and hard, and was aimed not at reward but at communion. This is how Dorothee Sölle, German peace activist, elucidates the meaning of such a response:

> [It] means entering into the struggle against the prevailing cynicism. It means being more and more free of fear. It means affirming the great "Yes." It means renewing and making true the old confidence which perhaps shone

into our childhood. It means loving God with all our hearts and all our souls and all our minds, without any reservation, without saying "Yes, if you give me this and that," and without saying, "But you once . . ." *It is a "Yes" without ifs and buts.* It is the great "Yes." (Italics ours.)[4]

It is possible for us to offer God a "yes" without "ifs and buts." No matter the course our lives have taken thus far, no matter how many questions remain, we can come to the point where we unequivocally say,

> Yes, God, I return your embrace. I may not know how to do this or what it means, but I want to learn to be more fully open to your love and be a conveyor of it to others.

When we are ready, like Teilhard, we can mark our "yes" with a personal *prayer of consecration.* As psychiatrist Gerald May notes in *The Awakened Heart,* the word *consecration* comes from the Latin roots *com,* "with," and *sacer,* "sacred." It implies "intentionally participating with the divine. We can be dedicated to anything: to a task, a cause, a nation. But we can be consecrated only to God."[5] May continues:

> Consecration means consciously participating in love, intentionally opening ourselves to accept the divinely given gift. It requires that we trust more in grace than in our personal capabilities. It calls for an attitude of willingness, a giving of ourselves to a power greater than our own.[6]

Thus, a prayer of consecration is the articulation of our response to God's reaching-out love. Our awareness of this love may have grown gradually or occurred suddenly. If we mark our consecration with prayer, we bring our response to a conscious level and attempt its expression in words.

For the disciple Peter, it was simply his words spoken to Jesus, "I love you." It took some wrestling with his own lack of love to come to this point. After Jesus' arrest, it was Peter who denied that he ever knew Jesus. This was, in effect, abandonment of the one he loved. It was only when Peter experienced Jesus reaching out to him again that he was able to state his love for all to hear (John 18:15–27 and John 21:15–17).

Thomas Merton, after having lived a committed life in a monastery for five years, was struck with his own self-absorption. In his journal, he wrote, "The chief thing that has struck me today is that I still have my fingers too much in the running of my own life."[7] He then went on to confess:

> The first essential is missing. I only say I trust You. My actions prove that the one I trust is myself—and that I am still afraid of You."[8]

Fear of God is common and indeed a chief obstacle to our trust in God's love. "If I say 'yes' to God, I might be asked to do something I'm afraid to do."

What really are we afraid of? The God that Jesus revealed? Or a judgmental being who resembles a stern authority figure out of our past? Jesus had a very different experience of God. To him, God was like a good shepherd who wants the best for his sheep—in fact, abundant life (John 10:10). Among the ingredients of that life, according to Jesus, are forgiveness, the chance to start over with a clean slate, guidance, belonging to a person and a community, power to work with others effectively, and an increasing desire to see God's justice and compassion.

While recognizing whatever fear we may have, we can participate in the abundant life described by Jesus when we sink ourselves, fear included, more fully in God's love. This Merton did when he went on to consecrate himself (warts included) with this prayer:

> Take my life into Your hands, at last, and do what You want with it. I give myself to Your love and mean to keep on giving myself to Your love—rejecting neither the hard things nor the pleasant things You have arranged for me. It is enough for me that You have glory. Everything You have planned is good. It is all love. . . .
> Only save me from myself. Save me from my own, private, poisonous urge to change everything, to act without reason, to move for movement's sake, to unsettle everything You have ordained.[9]

A full response to God's love includes saying "yes" to God not only in peak moments of commitment, but each day, and in fact, each moment with a prayer you compose yourself such as:

> I greet you this day, God.
> Your glory shines in the sky.
> Trees reveal your beauty.
> Let me recognize you at my side
> and in each one I see.
> Infuse my day with your love.

With a simple prayer of that sort, we open ourselves to God's presence in all of life.

Minute-by-minute awareness of God's love grows in us as we "practice the presence of God," to use the phrase of Brother Lawrence, the medieval monk and kitchen helper, who amidst his pots and pans recognized God's presence everywhere. To practice, in this sense, means to return home to God's love whenever we are conscious of straying from it.

Living in such a relationship with God is like any close relationship. At times it will have deep meaning and power; at other times the relationship will be quiet or uneventful or even stormy. Some periods will seem nourishing; others will appear dry and empty. The important thing is to place ourselves daily in the presence of God and let God's love work in us.

Responding in love to God involves joining in God's love for each person including ourselves. Here the way can become less clear.

Sherry Ruth Anderson and Patricia Hopkins, two friends in California, studied the life stories of thirty women across North America who had found "a direct relationship with the divine or the real."[10] Their findings have relevance to men as well as women.

They discovered that it was necessary for the women interviewed to say a fundamental "yes" to themselves. This meant that they were led not so much by their commitment but by their questions. Indeed, it entailed saying "no" to some commitments previously made, "letting go of the security of thousands of years of traditional teachings," and trusting that what they themselves experienced as sacred was indeed sacred.[11] This was "a profoundly disruptive process."[12] Leaving the known for the unknown, they trusted inner authority to lead the way.

As they listened to themselves and trusted what they found, they experienced feelings of despair, rage, jealousy, helplessness. Such experiences, though unwelcome and often surprising, were vital to these women's growth. One woman said as she left a spiritual community in which she had lived for many years,

> Mystery doesn't mean only some grand, ecstatic thing. It means stumbling around in the darkness, terrified that

nothing will be there if you don't call on God in the old way. Once I knew what my life was consecrated to and what my direction was. Now I don't know, and I don't even know where to look.[13]

Working through periods of self-questioning led the women to new levels of self-confidence and trust in God. Maria Rifo departed from her native Chile to settle in Albuquerque. Attracted at age sixty to Cesar Chavez's organizing of farm workers, she left her job in New Mexico to help Chavez in Delano, California. There she learned to do things she never thought she could do. After twelve years with the United Farm Workers of America, she told Anderson and Hopkins:

> The main thing that had happened to me in those twelve years was that I had come to believe in myself. You have to believe in yourself and then you can be merciful with everybody. I think this is what Jesus said.[14]

Saying "yes" to self, others, and God means saying "no" to what deflects us from that love, even though it may have been helpful at one time. Or it may involve saying "no" to new, enticing possibilities that seem off the mark for us when considered more deeply. And it may simply mean saying "no" to some of the seemingly harmless things we have allowed to take over large areas of our lives, keeping us perpetually and cheerfully distracted from the deeper invitation God is extending.

The question addressed in this book is, "How can I nourish my spirit?" Part of the answer is to begin with a firm commitment to open ourselves to the Spirit.

For some, commitment may have been a bad experience. Our commitments may have led us into dark periods of pain, or have resulted in betrayal. If our past experience has wounded us, we may be wary of commitment altogether and feel unable to make one now, even to God. That is understandable. But we do not have to remain stuck there. Betrayal and woundedness, potent themes in the biblical account, lead to a bigger picture if we are open to it. We address the questions the woundedness raises and look for the truth betrayal reveals. The hurt sustained can educate us in making a wiser choice the next time.[15]

The invitation to live an abundant life with God has been issued. It calls for our response. When we make that a wholehearted "yes" to God, ourselves, others, and all creation, we open ourselves to the solid nourishment God wants to give us.

GROUP DESIGN

Purpose: To share experiences of growth, hopes and questions about the course, and to examine the power and freedom that come with commitment decisions.

Materials: $8\frac{1}{2}$ x 11 sheets of paper, marking pens, newsprint.

A. Gathering Time, Large Group (*thirty-five minutes*)

To prepare for this and our subsequent sharing in small groups, take a sheet of paper and a marking pen, and in five minutes draw a picture or use a word to symbolize these:

✤ *a person, book, or event that has spurred your growth* in the past;

✤ your *hopes* for this course;

✤ a *concern*, question, or resistance you have regarding this course.

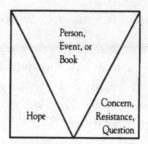

As an example, Dick's diagram is reproduced here. His father spurred Dick's growth by his encouragement and affirmation. He liked to hear Dick play the piano, so Dick depicted his father smiling, with some musical notes in the background. He hoped that being with others, feeling their support, and hearing their experiences would stimulate his own growth. So he drew a group of stick figures supporting one another. His concern was about time (Would he be able to give this the time it deserves?), so he drew a clock.

When everyone is ready, share your name (if you are new to each other) and describe the *person, event, or book that spurred your growth.* (You'll share hopes and concerns for the course in smaller groups.) Here is what Dick said: "My name is Dick Avella. I drew my father because he was always encouraging me. He especially enjoyed hearing me practice piano—that's why I put the notes there."

B. Sharing Groups (*twenty-five minutes*)

Move into groups of four with people you do not know well. Share names and phone numbers. Jot them in your notebook for ready reference. Then briefly share *hopes* and *concerns* for the course. You might want to write down key items by people's names so you can pray about these things.

C. Stories of Saying "Yes" and "No" (*forty-five minutes*)

The text for this session describes the value of saying "yes" to God's embrace and "no" to that which deflects us from it.

1. Each person take a few minutes to think about a positive experience of commitment, of saying "yes," in the life of someone you know. What were the particular aspects and effects of this "yes"? What were the "no's" that probably were said in order to say "yes"? (five of the forty-five minutes).

2. In twos (pairing with the person next to you), share your example, helping each other expand, go deeper, draw out the elements in each one (ten of the forty-five minutes).

3. In the large group, brainstorm: What are the characteristics of commitment, and what happens as a result of saying "yes"? Use only a word or a phrase, and record on a piece of newsprint (fifteen of the forty-five minutes).

4. Place the newsprint listing of commitment characteristics on the floor in the center of the group. Take a few minutes to reflect on how they illustrate the importance of saying a wholehearted "yes." Then ponder another dimension—how they illuminate this important fact: God has this kind of wholehearted commitment to us and invites us to respond with our "yes" individually and in company with others (fifteen of the forty-five minutes).

D. Closing, Large Group (*fifteen minutes*)

Choose one or two of the following suggestions as appropriate for your group:

1. Evaluate this session. (In a few words, what was helpful? What was not helpful?)

2. Sing a song familiar to the group.

3. Pray.

4. Discuss details of next session if necessary (time, place, leadership responsibility).

INDIVIDUAL WORK

Purpose: To examine our commitment to God, to express this by spending time regularly in God's presence, and to compose a personal prayer of consecration.

1. *Read:* Luke 9:57–62 describes the importance of commitment and reasons people hold back. Romans 12 is a picture of the committed life.

2. *Meditate and Write:* Using these Bible passages for background, write your response to these questions:

✤ What is the importance of commitment to God for me?

✤ What holds me back?

✤ In what way(s) do I want to say a more wholehearted "yes" to God? Try to be specific.

✤ Is there something to which I should say "no"?

3.   *Pray:* Write your own prayer of consecration to be used at the beginning of each day. *Bring this prayer to the group's next session.* Pray for the other members of the group and for your small group. Hold them and yourself in the committed love of God.

4.   *Summarize:* At the end of the week, summarize in writing your experiences, successes, failures, doubts, and joys as you worked with this material. Then read the text for Session 2 as a preparation for the next class.

SESSION 2

Listening

I know you believe you understand what you think I
said, but I am not sure you realize that what you heard is
not what I meant.[1]

In this sentence, Dody Donnelly sums up a dilemma we all
face: the difficulty of truly listening. Yet what an important tool
for growth it is! Three dimensions—listening to oneself, others,
and God—are integrally related to one another.

Listening is a way of loving, cherishing, and expanding our understanding of ourselves, others, and God. This session begins by
highlighting a few ways to listen to our inner world through paying
attention to our feelings, our dreams, and our bodies. Then we
consider listening to the outer world—other people, events, external reality. We conclude with thoughts about listening to God.

There are many ways to listen to our inner world. One is to
focus on our feelings and hear what they have to say. This may be
difficult. We may have learned that it is permissible to have and
share only "good feelings." "Bad feelings," such as jealousy, anger,
and resentment, may have been considered wrong and, perhaps,
even sinful. Thus, we may have denied their existence, suppress-
ing them so deeply that they cannot easily be recovered.

The Bible, however, portrays people who freely admitted all
kinds of feelings. The psalmists raged or exulted about their dis-
tress, joy, dread, being in the pits, climbing to the heights. Jesus
wept over his friend's death, reached in love to little children, and
overturned tables in anger at the violation of sacred space (John
11:32–38; John 2:13–17).

It is important to accept and listen to the honest feelings we have, no matter what they are. Feelings or passions contain energy; they give life its drive and verve. Just as surely as "love makes the world go round," so jealousy and anger have the power to stop the world, block human interaction, turn promising possibilities into deadly poison. Ideas and intellectual work are important, but it is feelings that give them power. One person can say, "God loves you" without feeling, and we are unmoved. Another may pour feeling into the same words, and we are gripped.

Another way to listen to our inner world is to pay attention to our dreams, discovering what they may be telling us about ourselves. We can approach them simply, in the way the Swiss psychiatrist Carl Jung did when he first began to use them in his work:

> . . . the patients would spontaneously report their
> dreams and fantasies to me, and I would merely ask
> "What occurs to you in connection with that?" or, "How
> do you mean that, where does that come from, what do
> you think about it?"[2]

Questions such as these open us up to parts of ourselves hidden from our conscious lives, areas that need attention, further development.

Our bodies convey important messages to us. A heart attack sounded an alarm for Ed. Fortunately, it was not too serious, said his doctor, but only if he would change his ways. Giving up his cigars and sugary breakfast cereal, Ed started a healthy diet, combining it with brisk daily walks. Now trim and vigorous, Ed says, "I wish I had started living like this years ago. I feel great!"

Our bodies need at least forty-five minutes of fresh air daily. Those who heed this make time, rain or shine, to be outdoors and thrive when they do so. Our bodies let us know what they need. And when we pay attention, our spirits are fed as well.

In earlier times it may have been easier to hear the messages of our bodies. There was less external stimulation (radios, boom boxes, televisions, telephones) to mask the inner signals. Our pace of living was slower. We could pay attention to our physical selves more readily.

When we do listen well, we discover the signs of well-being or dis-ease, and more easily trace these to their cause. In this way, we are helped to know what is right for us, psychologically as well as physically, in our work lives and relationships.

A number of approaches can help us learn to listen to our bodies. Yoga, massage, dance, and other forms of movement are just a few.

Journal keeping is a useful tool for tracking the messages of our feelings, dreams, and bodies. There are various ways to use this tool. Some people record feelings, dreams, or body sensations, jotting them down as they occur. This simply provides a container but may not teach us the meaning of these inner events. Ira Progoff has pioneered a unique way of teaching people to write, organize, and learn from their reflections. Instead of simply jotting down feelings as they occur, we make an additional effort to keep track of one feeling—anger, for example—and make an entry every time it occurs. Then we look back on the entries and try to understand them more fully. What situations or persons provoked anger? Is there a reason? Is there another way to approach this problem? Does the anger point to a positive energy that might be frustrated or unused but could be tapped in a creative way?[3]

Listening to ourselves enables us to listen more deeply to others and to give and receive nourishment by this contact. To give our attention to another person is hard work. It is important to listen carefully and make sure we have heard the message intended. An easy way to check this is to repeat what was said in our own words. The other person can affirm or correct our impression. A technique like this can sometimes seem artificial, but if used with an honest desire to understand it can clear up misunderstandings before they escalate. It also is a way of caring deeply for what the other is saying. Further, it can check our tendency to rush to the other's aid with advice, opinions, or solutions. When we listen with care and attention, we allow the person to share the first layer of awareness and then that which lies beneath.

To listen in this way is an act of love. Thomas Hart, teacher and counselor, puts it this way:

> To listen attentively to another and to go with another in companionship are expressions of love. To do either without love is an empty gesture and bears no fruit. . . . In my own years of receiving spiritual direction from various directors, it is clear to me that those who helped me the most were not the eldest of them, the holiest, or the best schooled in counseling and spiritual direction; it was those who loved me the most. How did it work? They enabled me to believe in myself, to rejoice in my own being and gifts, to accept the mystery of my life in hope, and to make the most of it. Compared to this, analysis, advice, summaries of treatises, and exhortations to the heights come to very little.[4]

Businessman Don McDermott calls this type of listening "listening with your heart." This means relating to and understanding the feelings of the other person. It was when his wife of twenty-seven years left him that he learned the importance of this way of listening.

> My wife had been trying all these years to talk to me about things that bothered her and . . . I was always analyzing . . . and giving solutions (as I did so well at work), rather than listening and understanding.[5]

McDermott started practicing "listening with the heart" with
a few close friends and a daughter, and found: "My whole relationship with these people changed almost instantly . . . The relationships became closer."[6]

Our listening encompasses more than other people. We need to
hear the messages of our natural world and of local and global
events. Having a sense of history, doing background reading, devel-
oping a value system, talking with people whose impressions we
trust—all these help us listen sensitively to our world and decide
how we are to live in it. A discerning heart helps us live with balance, relating with appreciation to the variety and beauty around
us, being fed by the rhythms of the seasons, our rich and varied cul-
tures, even the social and political challenges of our time.

What about listening to God? Sometimes we pray but seem
not to hear anything in return. If we do all the talking, often going
over the same problems repeatedly, our prayer is a one-way communication.

As in any intimate relationship, it is possible for our relationship with God to have give and take. What is called *listening
prayer* is a way to cultivate this. We bring ourselves to God as we
really are, our thoughts and feelings, being honest and open. This
is the background against which we can use the following steps to
listen for what God would say to us:

First, as in all listening, be present, with your whole being.
Settle down, relax, perhaps jot down any preoccupations for later
attention, collect yourself, and be still. Enter into a place of silent
waiting deep within. Members of the Society of Friends refer to
this place as the Divine Center or the Light Within. Listen to
Thomas Kelly's description of it:

> Deep within us all there is an amazing inner sanctuary of
> the soul, a holy place, a Divine Center, a speaking

Voice, to which we may continuously return. . . . It is a dynamic center, a creative Life that presses to birth within us. It is a Light Within which illumines the face of God.[7]

Second, nourish that center, your soul, by using a short Bible passage or some other appropriate material. Savor a small chunk, a phrase or a verse, turning it around, putting one of your life situations or that of another alongside it, and let it trigger new thoughts, feelings, or insights.

Third, communicate or converse with God. Sometimes this communication will be wordless, simply a time of basking in God's presence, "abiding in" God, as Jesus put it. In addition to this, if you need a word or guidance, ask for it. Simply say, "This is troubling me, God. What can you tell me about it?" Then listen in stillness. Perhaps a word, a feeling, an image, or an insight will come. Consider jotting it down for further pondering. Nothing may occur; the dialogue cannot be forced. Yet God has a way of getting through eventually if we are truly open and ready to hear. The response may take the form of deeper understanding, a lightened load, guidance, comfort, or challenge. All these happen to those who make listening to God a part of their lives.

Listening is a way to deepen our life with God, ourselves, and others. Difficult though it is, learning to listen is important. Although many techniques are available for sharpening our listening skills, perhaps most important is the desire to develop a "listening heart," an attitude of openness to and genuine appreciation of the wonder of life as it exists within and around us.

Note: For a summary of suggestions on listening, read the additional section "On Listening" (placed after the Group Design and Individual Work). This would be good to do before your group session on listening.

GROUP DESIGN

Purpose: To learn the importance of listening as a tool for growth and to practice listening to one another.

Materials: Newsprint.

A. Gathering Time, Large Group (*twenty minutes*)

Open the group in any way you like. If you want to have some fun, try one of the familiar children's listening games such as "Gossip." (In "Gossip," someone whispers a ridiculous and slightly complicated sentence in the ear of the next person, who in turn whispers it to the next one. This is repeated around the circle until the end, when you compare the last version to the first.)

B. Sharing Groups (*twenty minutes*)

In sharing what you did with the suggestions for Individual Work, it is not necessary to cover every item thoroughly. You may simply touch on some selected points. Remember to review good sharing practice:

✛ Speak about what is pertinent, personally important, current.

✛ Don't dominate the group. Give each person a chance to share briefly.

✛ If there is time, go back for further discussion.

We suggest that in this session you share what was life-giving and what was unproductive in your experience with the

Individual Work for Session 1. Following that, consider closing with the prayers of consecration you wrote.

C. Listening to One Another (*sixty-five minutes*)

What follows are the instructions for an exercise in listening that has been widely used in groups to teach skills in communicating, listening, and observing.

Note to the leader: It might help to ask at least two individuals to familiarize themselves ahead of time with the details of this exercise so they can help set it up during the session.

1.   Mention the value of listening to others, recalling some elements of good listening noted in the text. Make a few points briefly, perhaps with the section "On Listening" in hand.

2.   Move into groups of three. Extra people may join a group to make a foursome. The leader can facilitate this to make sure no one is left out.

3.   Set up the exercise with one sharer, one reflector, and one observer. Read these descriptions of your roles:

Sharer: Briefly share a problem (no more than five minutes). Discuss something that really concerns you—an area with unresolved feelings (positive or negative) that are not overwhelming. For example: leftover feelings from the last session, specific concerns about work or career, interpersonal relations, a pressing social issue. It should contain personal, unresolved, confusing feelings.

Reflector: Reflects back in own words what he or she has heard.

Sharer: Amplifies, clarifies, corrects wrong impressions.

Reflector: Reflects back again. Do this for three or four rounds.

Observer: Speaks about how each did in relation to learning/sharing suggestions, telling the Reflector and Sharer what seemed helpful, on target.

4. If time permits, exchange roles and repeat the process.
5. Large-group sharing.

   a. Informal feedback from observers: What happened?

   b. Brief discussion of ways to improve our listening skills.

D. Closing, Large Group (*fifteen minutes*)

Choose one or two of the following suggestions as appropriate for your group: evaluation of the session, discussion of details for next session, song, prayer. Suggestion for prayer: In keeping with the session on listening, be in silence together. Allow silence to come over you as a group. You may notice a deeper resting in silence as you relax into it, moving through and beyond the random noises nearby. After a suitable time, someone close by saying "Thank you" or "Amen."

INDIVIDUAL WORK

Purpose: To focus on the art of listening to God, self, and others.

A number of suggestions are presented. You may want to deal with them all, or concentrate on one or two.

1. *Listening to God:* Use the following three steps which have been discussed in the session text to cultivate this art.

   ✦ *Prepare:* Collect yourself, become quiet and relaxed. Let silence happen around and within you. Be in touch with an inner center of stillness where God may be met. As preparation for listening to God, focus on being present, at rest but alert, and attentive. If you can, devote several minutes to this quieting which is, in itself, a form of prayer.

✛ *Read the Bible:* Use a bit of Scripture, or other appropriate reading, as spiritual nourishment. This week we suggest Luke 8:40–56 and Luke 18:35–43. Each day be aware of how Jesus listened and was present to the people who approached him.

✛ *Pray:* In the quiet, picture the listening, caring Jesus with you. Tell him what is on your mind and listen for his response. It may be helpful to record what occurs in your journal.

2. *Listening to self: Describe* in writing a feeling that is of high intensity. Do this as fully and freely as possible. Then stand back and *reflect* in writing on the feeling. What made you feel this way? Why? What can you learn about it? How can its energy be tapped?

3. *Listening to others:* Read "On Listening," following item 4. Focus on the suggestions that are most pertinent, seeking concrete ways to try them as you listen to others this week.

4. *To prepare for the next session:* At the end of the week, write a brief summary of your personal work with the assignment. Then read the text for Session 3 as a preparation for the next class.

✛ On Listening ✛

A simple Australian bushman said to Sir Hubert Wilkins (the Arctic explorer) in his Pidgin English, "You set down quiet and listen alla time and eyes belong you lookabout see everything. Allabout feel quiet inside when with you."

From this lovely statement, we can catch the image of one who has so fully absorbed the skills of being present and listening that he brings peace to those around him. How does this happen? What can we do to attain it?

A few tips for growth in listening have come to our attention through readings and experience. Let's start with the *don'ts* (which most of us *do!*).

1. *Don't interrupt*. The greatest gift is to offer our attention.

2. *Don't probe*. Our questions should be ones of gentle encouragement rather than ones to satisfy our own curiosity. Some samples: "How did you feel then?" "What happened next?" "Can you explain that a bit more?" "Have you said all you'd like to say about this?" Other questions can be used to gain enough information to understand the problem or to help the other person think more deeply about the situation.

3. *Don't give advice:* We undermine others when we try to solve their problems.

4. *Don't judge*. Accept what others say as their perception.

5. *Don't sympathize sentimentally*. This can divert the focus of the speaker.

There are positive techniques for listening to add to our don'ts. Just to *be* there with the other is to give affirmation and a positive feedback. A good listener hears more than just the words. There may be body language communicating anger, fear, anxiety, confusion, bewilderment, hopelessness. To relate back to the other what we hear is clarifying; it helps us avoid misinterpretation and lets the other realize what he or she has said, perhaps opening the door to a deeper understanding of the situation.

The good listener may add the dimension of prayer, spoken or silent, as the greatest gift of all, recognizing the loving Spirit of God present in all situations.

SESSION 3

Recalling Our Stories

When English writer Evelyn Underhill wanted to sink her roots in deeper spiritual soil, she sought out scholar and spiritual director Friedrich von Hügel. The counsel he gave speaks to us all:

Find the way best suited to you.[1]

A primary tool for discovering our particular way to God is to look at our life stories. There we will find sources of spiritual power that are uniquely ours. This session helps us recall our stories and reflect on their meaning.

Our own life story may be the last place we look for spiritual insight. We might feel that the lives of others have more to tell us than our own. Biblical figures, heroes, and saints have been held up to us for emulation. Yet, their circumstances were different from ours, and their wisdom, while valuable, will take us only so far.

Do you wonder if your life story could be revelatory? You are not alone. Some years ago eighteen members of an Episcopal church in Washington, D.C., were selected at random for an inquiry by researcher Jean Haldane. Her purpose was to encourage each person to share his or her story. These she recorded and then studied. Her findings were striking:

1. With her gentle encouragement, each person revealed a fascinating pilgrimage shaped by personal history and crises. And in each story there was spiritual content, even though those interviewed had different ways of expressing it. This refuted the common observation that some people are spiritual and others are not.

2. All the participants found it helpful, life-giving, and exciting to share their journey, even though in their church people

normally did not "talk about religion." The myth that people resist speaking about their faith was exploded. In the presence of an
encouraging person who was genuinely interested, and away from
those who might judge the story or compare it with others, people
were deeply grateful for the chance to talk about their lives.

3. The people had not thought of sharing their story in
church or with anyone connected with their church. In what
would seem the natural place for people to share spiritual experience, the opportunity to do so never occurred.

4. No one connected with the church had asked any of the
project participants about their spiritual journey. This simply was
not a topic of conversation.

5. Through the process of sharing their stories with Jean,
participants reflected on their journeys and frequently discovered
next steps to take. This produced a clarity of direction that was
empowering. The interviewees did not need to be told what to do
next to continue their spiritual journey. Rather, in the freeing cli-
mate of the interview, many knew what to do.[2]

Remembering our stories is not new. The Bible was written by
people recalling their stories. Since biblical times, our tradition
has continued to hand down stories of individuals and communities who chose to be God's people. We see our lives mirrored in
their stories, and draw wisdom from the experience of those who
have gone before us.

One way to picture an overview of our life stories is to draw a
map of the main events: jobs, life decisions, significant people
known. On this map, we can indicate times when we were especially aware of God's presence or absence. This gives at a glance
a visual picture of the ups and downs of our journey, and in itself
leads to insights. A further step is to describe our map to another
person, a process which can bring us even greater clarity.[3]

Drawing a map prepares us for a more detailed way of recalling our story. We suggest in our workshops that the participants

write their spiritual autobiography. Initial reactions to such a suggestion range from: "What a wonderful opportunity!" to "You've got to be kidding—I hate to write!" Yet, with a little encouragement, people overcome their resistance, and in writing their story learn a great deal about their particular way of adhering to their own deep truth.

In the Individual Work following the text, we invite you to write your own spiritual autobiography. As you read the rest of the chapter, let the suggestions and stories stimulate your memory. Then set aside time to allow your memories to take shape in writing, letting the structure of your own life reveal itself.

You may want to begin with memories of childhood, neighborhood, family, and friends. Meinrad Craighead, an artist from New Mexico, remembers summers spent with grandparents in Little Rock:

> My grandparents didn't have much money, so it certainly wasn't that we kids were given lots of toys or taken places, but we had the land and we had our ingenuity. It was the only respite I had from Chicago where everything was pavement and even the apartment houses seemed regimented.[4]

What do you remember of the good times and hard times of your past? In what ways were you free to be yourself as a child, and how were you pressed to fit a mold? As a jog to memory, you might draw a sketch of yourself as your parents wanted you to be and as you really were inside. Then compare the two. The Swiss psychiatrist Carl Jung was conscious that at an early age he thought of himself as having two personalities:

> One was the son of my parents, who went to school and was less intelligent, attentive, hard-working, decent, and clean than many other boys. The other . . . was close to

nature, the earth, the sun, the moon, the weather, all living creatures, and above all close to the night, to dreams, and to whatever "God" worked directly in him.[5]

Did you have a similar inner and outer personality? What were they like?

Consider the mix of solitude and community in your life, those times when you sought your own space and when you kept company with others. Have you had special places that were yours? One of the women interviewed by Sherry Anderson and Patricia Hopkins for their study on women's spirituality recalled her difficult upbringing: "I kept trying to figure out how there could be a God when life seemed so excruciatingly unfair," she said. When asked who raised her, she replied,

> You really want to know who raised me? It was a pep-pertree at the end of our block, that's who raised me. It had a great nest inside that was like a womb. . . . You could sit in that womblike space and look out at the world without the world seeing you. . . . I felt safe and loved and protected in that tree. It was my link with God/creation—with what was stable and real.[6]

What have been your links with God and creation? Can you trace them as you allow your story to tell itself? In what ways have you been conscious of God's presence or absence? What images of God, or ideas and feelings about the divine have been important at different periods? Were there people in your life who helped you connect with God? In this regard, sociologist Elise Boulding remembers a pastor and his wife, her Sunday-school teacher:

> The pastor's wife took me aside one day and asked if I would like to come into her class. . . . She sensed that here was someone longing to learn what she was longing to teach! . . . Reverend Northwood and his wife were

both pastors in the truest sense of the word. They had a calling to make God's presence real for others. I don't recall that Reverend Northwood had any special oratorical gifts, but his sermons always held me completely because I felt he *knew* God.[7]

Did you have hopes and dreams about your work life? To what extent have they been realized? Have you succeeded in the way you had hoped? Or have you redefined success a number of times? Futurist Marilyn Ferguson quotes a businessperson's musings on success:

> I used to define myself in terms of specific accomplishments. Success might be an A in school—later it was business deals. Now success has to do with living my life in harmony with the universe.[8]

What disappointments have you sustained as you have gone about your work? In what ways has your view of work changed?

At age fifty-one, Elise Boulding came to what she described as her "upside-down turning." A visit to India confronted her with physical deprivation as she lived among people on the edge of life. Returning home, she welcomed a teenager in emotional crisis to stay with her and her family. The young man was in agony as he tried to get off drugs. She wrote:

> Watching his suffering, knowing that in a certain way I was as trapped and helpless as he, I suddenly one night saw myself as a small frog in the bottom of a deep well, leaping/leaping to get up and over the side. All my life I had been leaping. I knew where the sun was, I knew which way to jump, I knew there *was* an outside—another place to be. Yet I kept falling back into the bottom of the well.[9]

In that moment Elise Boulding's life passed before her. Suddenly she recognized "how we had all chained ourselves to daily rhythms that were bound to defeat us."[10] Unexpectedly, those chains snapped. "This was a kind of death—the death of that old try-hard frog, the birth of a new creature who found her way over the top of the well."[11] Met by God's grace, she sprang up, free.

Such vivid images for a moment of change! How would you describe the changes that have shaped you? Or the turning points, roads taken or left unexplored? Have you had moments of reckoning when you saw that things were not working in your life and change was thrust upon you? In what ways has grace broken through?

In describing his life, Robert Raines, director of Kirkridge retreat center in Pennsylvania, uses the image of leaving home, living in tents, being reborn, and going home. In his forties, he recognized that, like a sailing ship, he was being cast out to sea, "out of the safe haven and harbor" of the life he had built. He writes:

> I couldn't make sense of what I knew I had to do. The faith system that had served me so well, or which I had served so well for so many years, was no longer adequate to guide me. In a new and dark way I was on my own.[12]

He likened his transition time to living in tents, temporary structures that could be constantly moved. Relationships, work, faith—all seemed tentlike. Finally, he emerged a new person, one who began to locate his deepest authority in the depths of his own experience. He began valuing more parts of himself—anger, resentment, grief, sexual energy.[13] He opened himself more to the left-out people in society—political prisoners, the unemployed, the divorced, gays and lesbians. Listening to their pain, he joined with them in dispelling the forces that intensify their suffering.[14]

In what ways have you left home, lived in the wilderness, found new life, and returned? What people have widened your understanding? Which parts of yourself or society have you learned to befriend?

These questions and examples are meant to help you recall your journey. Each person's story is unique, creating its own patterns. As one woman said, "My life is like a crazy quilt."

Let your writing flow. As you remember the steps of your path, you will relive the highlights. That will position you to learn from the sweep and fullness of your life thus far, to thank God for its blessings, and to bring to God areas that need further healing (the subject of the next session). You may wish to ask God, "How have you been present in my life? What do you want to teach me through it?" With this perspective you may feel more clearly guided in your own way to the future.

At the end of his spiritual autobiography, Robert McAfee Brown wrote:

> The particular story that I have been telling does not end with a tidy conclusion. In fact, it does not end at all. That is the nature of the Christian story, too. It goes on. The book is never finished. We simply begin a new chapter. That is why the journey is occasionally terrifying, fulfilling, and always exciting.[15]

As you recall the roles of other people in your story, we invite you to hold them in prayer. Prayer for others is commonly called *intercession*. It is from a Latin root and means to act between parties, to mediate. We feel so strongly about intercessory prayer that we have built in an opportunity to experience it. If you are using this book as a course, the Group Design suggests that you share your life map with one other person. The Individual Work then invites you to pray for one another as you write your autobiographies.

Intercessory prayer was important to Jesus. He pledged his prayer for his friend saying, "Simon, I have prayed for you that your faith may not fail" (Luke 22:32). And Jesus asked others to pray for him, for example, in the garden before his death. The apostle Paul paints a wonderful picture of the risen Jesus praying for us all when he writes: "Christ died for us, Christ rose for us, Christ reigns in power for us, Christ prays for us" (Rom. 8:34, Phillips).

Paul points to an astounding truth. Not only was intercession important to Jesus in the past, it is a vital part of his relationship with each of us now. He cares about us so much that he is praying for us, for our loved ones, for people in the remotest places on Earth, for all people. There is a steady stream of the kind of committed love that intercession represents coming to us daily from Jesus.

Not only is this steady love available to us from Jesus, we can join him in this vital outpouring, becoming intercessors with him, joining our prayer to his universal prayer. What a fantastic invitation!

Sometimes we respond joyfully. We intercede with confidence, holding people who come to our attention "in the Light," as the Quakers say. But at other times, this is plain hard work, something we are committed to but which does not come easily. Whatever our frame of mind, we are invited to bring people before God for whatever God wants to give. We try to do this with an open spirit, trusting God's ultimate wisdom and love. To instruct God about what to do with a person is to think we know what is best.

A Scottish woman, Irene Glass, has been dedicated to intercessory prayer for many years. When asked what she does when she doesn't know how to pray for someone, she replied,

> That often happens to me, because people ask me to
> pray for difficult and puzzling situations. This is what I

do. I think about Jesus. He seemed to handle each person who came to him with superb sensitivity and effectiveness, and you'll notice that he never did quite the same thing with people. Each situation was unique. What I do is bring the person I am praying for to Jesus. I trust in his ability to know just what is right for that person. I tell him that I don't know, and that I want to put that person completely in his hands. And it's funny how often particular ways of praying for a person do come to me and I focus on them.

Praying for others is a beautiful gift. There are many ways to do it. Like the Quakers, you may hold people in the Light, or, with Irene Glass, bring people to Jesus. You may have other ways that you have discovered or will find. By praying for others we come to know our oneness with them more deeply and together are fed by the spring of God's love.

GROUP DESIGN

Purpose: To remember and share portions of our life story that have meaning for us.

Materials: Colored marking pens, newsprint or legal-size sheets of paper, words for song (see E, Closing).

A. Gathering Time, Large Group
(*twenty-five minutes*)

If time allows, open your session by having each person respond to the following questions.

✤ Where did you live as a child?

✤ How did you heat your home?

✤ What was the center of warmth for you (a person, place, pet, etc.)?

B. Sharing Groups (*twenty minutes*)

Remember what you did with the Individual Work on listening. Share one thing that had power and meaning for you and one thing with which you had difficulty.

C. Remembering Your Story (*thirty-five minutes*)

Drawing your Life Map: For this exercise, each person needs two marking pens of different colors and a piece of newsprint. Find a comfortable place where there is room to spread out and write. If colored pens are not available, differentiate the depiction of life events from one's spiritual journey by using a solid line for one and a dotted line for the other.

Note to the leader: Before beginning, it may help some people to see an example of such a map which is passed around or held up before the group. There is one on page 54 of this session. You or someone who volunteers and has prepared ahead of time should read aloud the following instructions:

"We're going to do an exercise that will help us listen to our past. Take two marking pens of different colors and a piece of newsprint.

"As a first step, take one color and represent your *life events* by drawing a line on the paper from left to right, moving up and down, using a curved or jagged line. Proceed with drawing the line as I read these instructions and we think together of the events from our earliest memories to the present. Use symbols of your own choosing to indicate special events and how they affected you. For example, perhaps you might represent the birth of a sister by a dark cloud, or moving to a new house by a sunburst. Or use plus and minus signs or a happy face or frowning face.

"Begin your line by making an 'x' on the left-hand side of the paper about midway from top to bottom. Draw the line forward slowly to the right, and let it represent the feelings you have about your *preschool years*. Were you happy, secure? Were there illnesses, traumas? (*Pause*.)

"Then make a mark indicating the *start of school* and a visual reminder of your feelings then—frightened, excited, disappointed, confident. (*Pause*.)

"As you remember your *elementary school years*, think of how active or quiet you were, of your friends, your teachers, and others who played important roles. Indicate that stage of life on your paper. (*Pause*.)

"Mark your *adolescent period* and remember your feelings about friends, dating, acceptance, hard adjustments, any deaths in your immediate circle, adventures, accomplishments. Indicate these on your paper. (*Pause*.)

"Mark the time you *left home* for work or school and your feelings then about independence and your sense of purpose or lack of it. (*Pause*.)

"Then mark important events *after schooling*: marriage—smooth and rough spots; career changes; travel; financial stress or security; children; illnesses; changes in direction—successes, failures. (*Pause*.)

"Now, *as a second step*, take the other marking pen, and with that we'll draw another lifeline, with particular attention to our relationship with God. We'll draw a new line on the same piece of paper, beginning from the same starting point, to show our spiritual journey as it unfolds in our lives. Again we can use fluctuations in our line or symbols to indicate the peaks and valleys of our spiritual experience.

"Begin with how you felt about God when you were a *child*— any times you were aware of God's loving care, presence, or absence. Was prayer a part of your life? Were family religious customs? Was church important to you? How? Let this period include preschool and elementary school years. (*Pause.*)

"Next, consider *adolescence*. Was that a time of turmoil, dryness, questioning? Did you have people with whom you could share? (*Pause.*)

"*Early adult years:* What was important then in your relationship with God? Did you feel near to or far from God? Were your concepts of God changing? Were you searching for God, or were you occupied with other things? (*Pause.*)

"*Up to and including the present:* What is happening now in your relationship to God? Do you feel more or less commitment than before? Do you have yearnings about your relationship with God that you could depict? Where is God for you as you are aware of aging in yourself and others? (*Pause.*)"

D. Sharing from the Life Map
(*twenty-five minutes*)

We suggest you do this in pairs, selected if possible from members of your permanent sharing group because you have built some rapport with them. If this does not work out for all, simply pair people for this part of the session. As you settle in your pairs for sharing, each person check two or three important happenings from your life map and spiritual journey that you would like to share. Then in the time allowed, go back and forth in your sharing—each describing one happening, and then listening to the other person's description. Share as freely and in as much detail as you wish (that is, one event in detail or several more briefly), but make sure each has about equal time.

Note: It is very easy for one person to take too much of the time as the other person in courtesy allows this to happen. Watch the time and divide it equally.

E. Closing, Large Group (*fifteen minutes*)

Choose one or two of the following suggestions as appropriate for your group: evaluation of the session, discussion of details for next session, prayer, song ("He's Got the Whole World in His Hands").

INDIVIDUAL WORK

Purpose: To make a deeper examination of our pilgrimage through writing our autobiography and to support one another with intercessory prayer as we do this.

1.   This week write your *spiritual autobiography*. Trust God's guidance in what you write, and record what comes. Don't worry about grammar, spelling, or "perfect" writing. Just begin at the beginning and let it flow. Content, not style, is what matters.

Write your autobiography on a paper separate from your journal. After the next session we will suggest that those who would like to share their autobiographies (or parts of them) do so with one other person. This is strictly voluntary. The main point for now is to write for yourself in a way that will be accessible to you in the future. Some of the questions in the session text may help you get started, but feel free to use your own format.

2.   For daily quiet time and for nourishment as you reflect on your own history, read Psalm 139. During each period of reflection, choose a phrase for meditation and journaling.

3.   During the week, practice intercessory prayer by being a specific intercessor for the person with whom you shared your life map. Pray that God's love may be revealed more clearly as they write their autobiography, and that the person will be enabled to respond anew to God's love. You may find inspiration in John 17:1–26. Jesus interceded for his disciples in a beautiful prayer just prior to his death. Christians have practiced this form of prayer ever since. How natural to want to support one another with spiritual help as well as physical and emotional help!

4.   *To prepare for the next session:* Write a brief summary of your personal work with the assignment. Then read the text for Session 4 as a preparation for the next class.

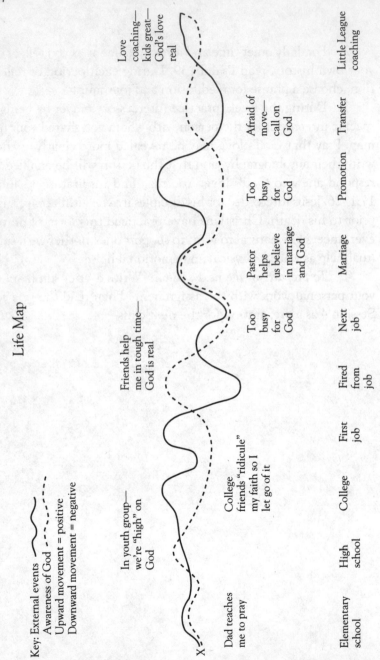

Life Map

Key: External events
Awareness of God
Upward movement = positive
Downward movement = negative

X

Dad teaches
me to pray

In youth group—
we're "high" on
God

College
friends "ridicule"
my faith so I
let go of it

Friends help
me in tough time—
God is real

Pastor
helps
us believe
in marriage
and God

Too
busy
for
God

Too
busy
for
God

Afraid of
move—
call on
God

Love
coaching—
kids great—
God's love
real

| Elementary school | High school | College | First job | Fired from job | Next job | Marriage | Promotion | Transfer | Little League coaching |

SESSION 4

Cleansing and Healing

When we are tired and grimy at the end of a day, a hot shower makes us feel clean. If a friend recovers from an illness, we are delighted. If someone has been estranged from loved ones and communication is somehow restored, that is good news. Cleansing, healing, restoration. Each is a cause for celebration.

In this session we look at how inner healing can be a regular part of our lives.

No wonder the first Christians in the Book of Acts were joy-filled as they shared the good news wherever they went. They were convinced that whoever felt soiled by sin could be forgiven and cleansed. Ailing or hurt people could be healed. And estrangement could be transformed into a deep sense of belonging. These blessings were available to anyone who believed in Jesus, the forgiver, healer, and restorer.

When we reflect on our past, as we do when writing our autobiographies, we notice times of grace and vitality but also roadblocks to growth. These may be resentments, apathy, destructive acts, attitudes of unforgiveness, or painful experiences that were never healed. Left unattended, they thwart further growth and infect our total well-being. Furthermore, this infection may spread beyond us to our immediate family and others we know. Surely we still need cleansing, healing, forgiving.

Healing and reconciliation were natural in the lives of the early Christians. They not only talked about healing and reconciliation, they were agents of healing themselves:

> Now many signs and wonders were done among the
> people by the hands of the apostles. . . . so that they

even carried out the sick into the streets, and laid them
on beds and pallets, that as Peter came by at least his
shadow might fall on some of them. The people also
gathered from the towns around Jerusalem, bringing the
sick and those afflicted with unclean spirits, and they
were all healed. (Acts 5:12, 14–16, RSV)

A major thrust of Paul's sermon at Antioch was to proclaim
Jesus as the one who forgave sins and to spell out the implications
of that for his listeners. J. B. Phillips translates the key point:

It is therefore imperative . . . that every one of you
should realize that forgiveness of sins is proclaimed to
you through this man. (Acts 13:38, Phillips)

A number of movements in the Christian churches help us
continue the early Christian practice of healing and reconciliation. The International Order of Saint Luke the Physician,
founded in 1953 by an Episcopalian priest, is open to those who
want to further Jesus' healing ministry by establishing healing services in churches, promoting pastoral and counseling services, cir-
culating literature, and fostering healing missions in large cities.

Using the new rite for confession, speaking face-to-face with
a priest, Roman Catholics find fresh power in the sacrament of
reconciliation. And in the sacrament of the anointing of the sick,
they lay hands on ill people, pray, and annoint them with oil, just
as was done by earlier Christians. Certain people such as Ruth
Carter Stapleton, Francis MacNutt, and Matthew and Dennis
Linn are called to the ministry of healing and have written helpful books based on their experiences.[1]

The Iona Community in Scotland, founded by George
McLeod, has brought back to life ancient prayers and rituals, particularly of the Celtic people. Their weekly healing services and

prayer circles have influenced others to move in this direction.[2]
For example, the Christian Fellowship of Healing in Edinburgh,
started by Church of Scotland people and supported by members
of other church bodies, maintains a ministry of healing, counseling, and prayer through its center and in individual churches that
have responded to its example.[3]

In a telling passage, Jesus related forgiveness of sins and healing of illness:

> Then some people appeared, bringing him a paralytic
> stretched out on a bed. Seeing their faith, Jesus said to
> the paralytic, "Courage, my child, your sins are for-
> given." And at this some scribes said to themselves,
> "This man is blaspheming." Knowing what was in their
> minds Jesus said, "Why do you have such wicked
> thoughts in your hearts? Now, which of these is easier:
> to say, 'Your sins are forgiven,' or to say, 'Get up and
> walk?' But to prove to you that the Son of Man has au-
> thority on earth to forgive sins,"—he said to the para-
> lytic—"get up, and pick up your bed and go off home."
> And the man got up and went home. (Matt. 9:2–7, JB)

Jesus saw that this person needed to be unbound from what
may have created fertile soil for illness. He extended forgiveness
as a first step. After that, healing took place.

Forgiveness is central to Christian community. Dietrich Bonhoeffer, German pastor in Nazi Germany, together with some
colleagues formed an underground seminary to prepare students
for both a pastoral and a prophetic role in that tragic time. While
pursuing academic studies, they formed a strong community of
prayer, fellowship, and daring action. An element that strengthened their community was the practice of confessing before a
brother or sister. Bonhoeffer chose one of his students, Eberhard

Bethge, as his confessor, and described the importance of this practice in his work *Life Together*.[4] He thought that no one person should hear the confession of everyone else in a community, but that each member should both hear and make confession before a brother or sister. This enabled the whole community to bear the darkness of its individual members. Everything was open to the light of honest human interchange and love. A depth of caring occurred that was impossible when hurts, resentments, and blocks to growth were hidden.

Agnes Sanford, Episcopalian laywoman, also has helped us understand and recover the healing ministry of Jesus. One of her contributions is the healing of memories. She believes that since Jesus is the same today as yesterday, it is possible for him to enter through our imagination into our past experiences and heal them. Our part is to open these memories to him and to visualize Jesus present, healing the hurt and restoring what needs mending.[5]

Open confession in the presence of another and prayer for the healing of memories are two of many tools that make forgiveness real and remove obstacles to growth. It is inspiring to see what happens when we try this. Using a guided meditation such as the one included in the Group Design, we visualize Jesus present, bring to him the hurt that needs healing, and open ourselves to the healing he offers. We might receive this through an image. For example, one participant in this meditation saw Jesus holding her and the person from whom she felt estranged, both enclosed in his loving arms.

Or we might be given something to do such as writing a reconciling letter to a parent. We might feel calmed or released from pain or tension. Or we may have no immediate experience but may find some benefit later.

What we have described is a simple process for reconciliation and healing:

1. Identify what needs healing.

2. Ask for healing.

3. Receive forgiveness and healing.

4. Carry out action that will further the healing process.

To make our experience of healing more tangible, it can be helpful to have a witness. This person might be someone who represents the community of faith. As Bonhoeffer discovered, a community is enlivened when healing and reconciliation are built into its life, when people recognize that everyone needs healing and forgiving, and when everyone not only offers confession but also acts as confessor. Ritual increases the impact of the healing experience because it reaches us on many levels of awareness. It can be as simple as taking another's hands, or offering a back rub, or marking the person with oil as did the early Christians.

Healing and forgiving were central to Jesus' life and ministry. He taught his disciples how to extend this unique way of loving. The community of faith has preserved prayers and practices for healing, restoring, and reconciling that are available for us and our communities. We can learn about them from others, but only as we try them out ourselves will they become real and vital for us.

GROUP DESIGN

Purpose: To share points of gratitude in our lives and to experience healing or forgiveness for what blocks our growth.

Materials: Candle, oil, small bowls or cups, small table, Bible, music with healing theme on record or tape.

A. Gathering Time, Large Group
(twenty minutes)

Since much of this session is quiet and meditative, start with something lively like some rousing camp or motion songs.

After song and movement, settle down in the large group for some journal writing in preparation for small-group sharing. Think about your life story as you worked with it this week. Jot down points of gratitude: people, events, situations for which you are thankful. Choose one or two items. Use a few minutes to expand your thoughts in writing. What made you grateful? Go into some detail. Relive in writing the good feelings associated with that moment. Explore your thankfulness.

B. Sharing Groups (twenty minutes)

1. Speak about how it was to write your autobiography and pray for your partner. Share ups and downs.

2. Share a point of gratitude with the group.

3. End with prayers of thanks for each other's lives.

C. Healing, Cleansing, Forgiving
(forty-five minutes)

Note to the leader: As part of this exercise, set up a worship center on a small table in the center of the group. Have on hand these items: a candle and matches (to be lit as you begin), a small container of oil, and additional containers for oil for each pair of people in the group. Add any other items that symbolize for you Christ's healing, cleansing, or forgiving love.

This exercise has three parts: preparation, guided meditation, and a cleansing liturgy. Each part should be led by the leader who will say the following (speak slowly, leaving lots of time for pauses):

Preparation: "In this session, we will *image* the healing Christ with us and *symbolize* this healing with oil as we pray together.

"To center ourselves, focus for a moment on our worship center, which is intended to create an atmosphere of prayer. As we look at the objects before us, let's remember that the lighted candle represents Christ's presence, and the oil his healing love.

"For grounding and encouragement, I invite us to recall silently instances when we have experienced Christ's healing for ourselves or others. (*Pause.*)

"Now let's speak briefly about a few of these experiences, describing what happened and what was important to us. (*Ten minutes for sharing healing stories.*)

"To prepare for our meditative imaging of the healing Christ, get comfortable with pen and paper at hand. Relax and become quiet. . . . In this meditation, periods of silence will alternate with time for journal writing. We will use our imaginations. The great masters of prayer frequently suggest imagining Christ present as a preparation for prayer."

Guided Meditation: "You may wish to close your eyes. Offer a prayer to be shown an area that needs healing and for trust in God's presence with you. Let an *area* come to mind *that needs healing, forgiving, reconciling, or cleansing.* It may help to think over your life map or your autobiography to identify a situation, person, attitude, or event which needs that attention. We'll use about three minutes for this. (*Pause.*)

"Now *imagine you are in a garden*—one you actually know or one created by your imagination. See the colors and forms; hear the sounds; smell the fragrance. Notice the landscaping, natural or well trimmed. Is there a bench? a path? Feel at home. Then imagine that Jesus is present with you. See him there. (*Pause for two or three minutes.*)

"*Speak with Jesus about the area* that needs healing. Say as much about it as you like. Then listen for Jesus' response. Record what happens in your journal. Ask Jesus to help you understand the situation as he does, and as do the others involved. Record your impressions. (*Pause for seven to ten minutes.*)

"Now ask Jesus for *what you want or need* in this situation, what you would like to have happen—for example, insight, forgiveness, healing. Try to be open to what Jesus wants to give you. (*Pause for two to three minutes.*)

"Next, ask Jesus to *show you what is needed now*—what he would have you understand, say, or do with regard to another person, your attitude, a situation. (*Pause for two to three minutes.*)

"Finally, bring your interaction with Jesus to a close, knowing you can return whenever you wish. Stretch. Stand."

D. Cleansing Liturgy (*Twenty minutes*)

As everyone is standing, remind people, if appropriate, of the meaning of the symbolic objects you are using. Then be seated in pairs (life map partners) facing each other.

The leader pours the oil into the small containers and gives each pair a container with instructions such as these: "Down through the ages, oil has been a symbol of

✚ healing (Jas. 5:14);

✚ the spirit (Isa. 61:1);

✚ cleansing (Luke 7:36–38; 10:34);

✤ strength (Ps. 89:20–22);

✤ joy, celebration (Ps. 45:6–8).

(*Read one or more of the suggested Bible passages if you like.*)
"Decide who will speak first. When it is your turn, mention to your partner the area for which you have sought healing. Do this as specifically or as generally as you like. (An example: 'I have asked for healing between me and a co-worker in the office.') If you prefer not to say anything, simply say so. The listener then anoints your hands with oil, touching them on the palms or the back. Then your partner may hold your hands and say a word of blessing or encouragement, such as 'Let us believe together that Jesus has healed you or is giving you the help you need.' Or he or she might say a brief prayer, such as 'We thank you, Jesus, that you helped people long ago and can do so today. Give John the help he needs.' If prayer aloud seems awkward, use a silent prayer."

During these prayers and blessings, there might be background music like "There is a Balm in Gilead," or another with a healing theme.

E. Closing, Large Group (*fifteen minutes*)

Choose one or two of the following suggestions as appropriate for your group: evaluation of the session, discussion of details for next session, prayer, song such as "Peace Is Flowing like a River."

INDIVIDUAL WORK

Purpose: To deepen our reception of healing, cleansing, or forgiveness and to ponder ways of extending that to others.

1. Ponder Luke 15:11–32 and Luke 23:32–43 to increase your awareness of the healing and forgiving love of God.

2.   Consider receiving a deeper or more extensive healing of your past or present. Become conscious of specific moments or areas of your life that need healing. Envision God's healing power restoring you to wholeness through Jesus.

3.   Is there a relationship in your life in which you are conscious of causing some hurt, distance, or brokenness? The relationship could be with someone living or dead. (Even though a person has died, change and growth can still occur in our understanding of the relationship.) Are there ways in which you can help restore wholeness to that relationship, either by forgiving yourself or the other, having a talk, making a phone call, or writing a note? Consider taking one such concrete step this week.

4.   *To prepare for the next session:* Write a brief summary of your personal work with this assignment. Then read the text for the next session.

SESSION 5

Living with a Generous Spirit

Actions speak louder than words. The actions of a Mother Teresa witness to the love of God as no words can. What can we do to demonstrate God's generosity through our life choices as strongly as she does?

In this complex world, answers are hard to discover. Unlike Mother Teresa, who has a single commitment to the dying of Calcutta, most of us have multiple commitments—to family, job, community, the Earth. In being faithful to all these commitments, how can we make choices about the way we spend money, the work we do, how we move about, and where we live that truly reflect God's generous love for all people? This is the question that this session addresses.

Jesus' familiar image of the vine can help us. "Abide in me," he says, "and you will 'bear much fruit'" (John 15:4, RSV). Immerse yourself in God's love and allow that love to guide all your decisions. First, be. Then, do.

Those who have tried to live this way testify to its power. One of these is the Quaker philosophy teacher Thomas Kelly, who crafted an essay entitled "The Eternal Now and Social Concern."[1] He writes that as we allow God's love to bubble up within our being, even in the midst of strife and hardship, we are infused with a cosmic love for all creation and guided in particular ways to embody this love.

> There is a tendering of the soul, toward *everything* in creation, from the sparrow's fall to the slave under the lash. The hard-lined face of a money-bidden financier is as

deeply touching to the tendered soul as are the burned-out eyes of miners' children, remote and unseen victims of his so-called success. There is a sense in which, in this terrible tenderness, we become one with God and bear in our quivering souls the sins and burdens, the benightedness and the tragedy of the creatures of the whole world, and suffer in their suffering, and die in their death.[2]

But, at the same time, God gives particular concerns to us as a focus for action and responsibility. Writes Kelly, "We cannot die on *every* cross."[3] In God's design, we do not have to do it all. We are given a part to play and what is needed to play that part well.

If I am economically poor like formerly homeless LeVerne Brewster in Washington, D.C., my part may be to address the survival needs of my family. That will guide my choice of work, living place, and community involvement. You will find me in the Homebuyers Club learning how to acquire and pay for a decent place to live. Or in a parents' group helping one another keep our kids safe from violence. To be fully productive, I must focus on appropriating for myself and my family more of society's resources.

On the other hand, if I, like Barbara and David Sorensen, have more of this world's goods than my fair share, I may need to consider limiting consumption. In their book, *'Tis a Gift to Be Simple*, the Sorensens report that two incomes were required for them to live in their house and keep up with expenses. "We felt overextended and out of control—in our money, in our time, in our spirits."[4] This led to some big decisions:

> We put our house on the market. We reduced our job commitments by half. We cut other things in half: mortgage, taxes, house size. A drastic move? Yes. A bit hasty?

Perhaps. But it allowed us the energy to breathe easy once again.[5]

They discovered how to live more with less. With less expenses came more time and energy, more freedom. This they used to be more attentive to God, more in communion with what really mattered. This led them to make choices about food, transportation, and clothes that promoted personal and global health.

Their promptings for change came from several directions—from listening to God in Scripture, from firsthand contact with people who live with very little, and from their bodies, which were sending messages—stress, headaches, low energy.

The Sorensens woke up, changed, and found themselves embracing a simpler life-style. They learned the difference between wants and needs and freed themselves from what ailed them. Describing what happened, Barbara writes, "It was fun because it was freeing. It changed our lives."[6]

No matter what our income and where we live, all of us, to preserve the planet, must embrace choices that promote global health. Asking "How Much Is Enough?" Worldwatch researcher Alan Durning puts forward an ecological Golden Rule:

> Each generation should meet its needs without jeopardizing the prospects of future generations to meet their own needs.[7]

Durning pleads for personal and political changes to move in this direction. The result of such efforts leads to a much more satisfying existence in the long run. He writes:

> In many ways, we might be happier with less. In the final analysis, accepting and living by sufficiency rather than excess offers a return to what is, culturally speaking, the human home: to the ancient order of family,

community, good work, and good life; to a reverence for excellence of skilled handiwork; to a true materialism that does not just care *about* things but cares *for* them; to communities worth spending a lifetime in.[8]

Thus, Durning presents the global necessity for living more with less.

When Jesus' promise of abundant life did not refer to having more things. Rather it invites us, according to writer Parker Palmer, to live out of an assumption of abundance, not scarcity.[9]

This is what Jesus did when feeding the crowd who had gathered around him. The disciples recognized that the people would be needing food in that lonely place. When Jesus asked his followers to feed the crowd themselves, they protested, "We have no more than five loaves and two fish" (Luke 9:13, JB).

Jesus suggested that the huge crowd of five thousand be invited to sit down in smaller groupings where they could relate face-to-face. Then Jesus took the small amount of food the disciples had, blessed it, and offered it to those around him. The report states that not only was everyone satisfied but that there were twelve baskets of leftovers!

In interpreting this passage, Palmer feels that the real miracle consisted in Jesus turning the disciples and crowd from operating out of the scarcity assumption, that there was not enough to eat, to the abundance assumption, that with generosity there was enough for all. As Palmer sees it, when sitting in smaller groups, the people related to one another in a friendly fashion, and inspired by Jesus' generosity in sharing the meager amount of food he and the disciples had, were moved to share what they had. In this way, each person received enough.

The children's song "Magic Penny" by Malvina Reynolds captures the essence of the assumption of abundance:

> Love is something if you give it away,
> give it away, give it away,
> Love is something if you give it away,
> you end up having more.
> It's just like a magic penny,
> hold it tight and you won't have any.
> Lend it, spend it, and you'll have so many,
> they'll roll all over the floor.[10]

When we find ourselves resistant or afraid to be generous with possessions or time, it may be that we have allowed ourselves to be ruled by the scarcity assumption. Scarcity says that if I give generous amounts of money to Greenpeace, I'll have less for my needs. Abundance assumes that the success of Greenpeace's efforts to promote good environmental stewardship will result in an abundance of clean air and water for my grandchildren.

The biblical principles of abiding in God's love and operating from that abundance provide general guidance for life choices. But for each specific decision about how to spend our time and material goods, we must open ourselves for particular guidance. This is where the *prayer of discernment* comes in.

In the sixteenth century, St. Ignatius of Loyola, founder of the Jesuits, developed a process to be used by individuals and communities when making significant decisions. This we can use today by ourselves or in the context of what is called a guided retreat, usually led by people trained in Jesus' spirituality. Here, in a general way, are the steps:

1. Consciously be in the presence of God.

2. Examine as objectively as possible the elements of the choice to be made.

3. Become aware of areas of unfreedom.

4. Make a tentative decision and live with it for a few days.

5. During this time note your inner state (peaceful or troubled).

6. Proceed as indicated by these fruits to remain either with your choice or to "try on" an alternative.[11]

Another form of discernment prayer is simply to ask God questions and then listen to what happens at that moment or as your life unfolds. Some questions we have used are:

✤ Who are the poor for me?

✤ What is my fair share of the world's goods?

Barbara and David Sorensen suggest these:

✤ What excess can I remove from life that will help me express my true values?

✤ What parts of my life's story are distractions that only keep me off pace and running ragged?[12]

Discernment is much broader than a process. It involves growing in God's loving way and seeking that with consistency. Over time we learn to determine more surely when we are living in harmony with God's Spirit and when we are not.

Life choices are both personal and public. Do I use the products of or invest in companies that exploit the Third World? Does having my own car make me callous to the need for better public transportation? Am I making my views known to public officials?

The need to examine life choices is ongoing. Our lives change as do the needs of the world. To rethink these decisions, consider building into your life a time to review such choices, to be newly confronted by changing realities and freshly converted to a more just response. This can be done by yourself or with a group.

Once we have made a decision, it is good to have support in following through. Communities of Benedictines for fifteen hundred years have supported one another in living the simple, balanced, and nourishing life described by St. Benedict. Three vows center them on God's love: *obedience*, interpreted as saying "yes" to God's infinite love and acting out of that; *stability*, accepting this place (where I am), this people as the way to God; and *conversatio morum*, or commitment to lifelong transformation as a follower of Jesus. To support one another in living these vows, St. Benedict composed a "rule of life" that spelled out in some detail how the vows translate into everyday living.[13]

Decisions about life choices may involve changing long-standing habits. That is why individuals and groups, whether or not they are in a monastic community, find it helpful to incorporate decisions regarding time, money, material possessions, home, and work, into a rule of life. Also called a spiritual plan or a nourishment plan, this helps us focus on what matters.

In whatever way we choose to bring our life choices into agreement with Jesus' values, we will find our spirits nourished. We will be living our vision, not simply dreaming about it. We will be people of hope in the sense meant by poet and former Czech president Vaclav Havel when he wrote:

Hope is a state of mind, not of the world . . .
It is an orientation of the spirit,
an orientation of the heart;
It transcends the world that is immediately
experienced,
and is anchored somewhere beyond its horizons.
Hope, in this deep and powerful sense,
is not the same as joy that things are going well,
or willingness to invest in enterprises that are

obviously heading for . . . success,
but rather, an ability to work for something
because it is good, not just because
it stands a chance to succeed.[14]

GROUP DESIGN

Purpose: To hear some Bible passages on life choices and to share contemporary stories of life choices that have meaning for us.

Materials: Bible, newsprint, marking pens.

A. Gathering Time, Large Group (*twenty minutes*)

Recently in the newspaper there was a photo of a woman refugee fleeing a troubled area and carrying a huge television set on her head. Was this her most prized possession? If you suddenly were in the same spot, what one item would you want to take with you? Take a few minutes in silence, and then each one share what you would take and why.

B. Sharing Groups (*twenty minutes*)

Give each person a chance to share one point about receiving healing, cleansing, or forgiveness through prayer and one point about extending forgiveness or healing to another. Or share one experience with the Individual Work that had positive value and one that presented difficulties.

C. Check-in Time on the Reading (*fifteen minutes*)

Review briefly the main points of the session text and share one way in which you felt challenged by the chapter.

D. Life-style Questions *(fifty-five minutes)*

1. *What the Bible says about life choices:*

   a. Read the following passages without comment, taking turns around the room (Note for the leader: consider assigning one or two passages per person in advance. Each will have marked the passages and will read them in turn):

Luke 16:13–15	Luke 14:12–14
Mark 1:16–20	Matt. 8:19–21
Matt. 19:21–22	John 2:6–10
Matt. 5:40–42	Luke 6:30
Luke 12:25	Luke 6:38
Luke 11:37–42	Mark 10:21–25
Luke 12:33	

   b. Large group sharing: What do these Bible passages say? What general guidelines do they present that can help us with life choices?

2. *What lives of individuals can tell us* about specific choices:

   a. On large pieces of paper put these categories:

money	time	home
work	life focus	
transportation	food	location
simplification	generosity	rule of life
regular review of life-style choices		

b. The way we handle each of these categories affects our life-style. Ask participants to place their initials beside categories that they could illustrate from real life—their own or others'.

c. *Sharing free-for-all:* Share as many stories as time permits, recognizing that there may not be time for all of them.

E. Closing, Large Group (*ten minutes*)

Choose one or two of the following suggestions as appropriate for your group: evaluation of the session, discussion of details for next session, prayer, song ("Simple Gifts").

'Tis a Gift to Be Simple

'Tis a gift to be simple, 'tis a gift to be free,
'Tis a gift to come down where we ought to be.
And when we find ourselves in the place just right,
'Twill be in the valley of love and delight.
When true simplicity is gained,
To bow and to bend we shan't be ashamed.
To turn, turn will be our delight,
Till by turning, turning, we come down right.

INDIVIDUAL WORK

Purpose: To consider decisions about life choices in the light of Jesus' values.

1. Read Luke 12:13–48. Jesus talks about seeking first the Reign of God as the focus of a person's life. How does that translate specifically into your life? What is your focus? What is your treasure? To what are you overly attached? What makes

you excessively anxious? Note your responses to these questions in your journal.

2.   Ask God specifically how to relate to the things of your life. Ask what life choices you need to address in order to express more faithfully the focus of your life. Are there changes to make? What are they? Pose these questions and then wait in silence for insights and openings that come from within you. Jot these down in your journal.

3.   Reflect on the generosity of God in your life. Then focus on your central concerns as described by Thomas Kelly. Experiment with one *concrete change* related to life choices this week. Examples: fast; give time or money; cut something out; cut back on car use; eat lower on food chain; take time for yourself; simplify; allow the replenishing, refreshing, aspect of God's creation to touch you; slow your pace; express your own creativity; call or write your congressperson on an issue that concerns you; take an action that expresses Jesus' values on a public issue. Write down your feelings, thoughts, and reactions.

4.   This week, focus on one aspect of a possible rule of life or spiritual nourishment plan for yourself—your relationship to the material aspects of your life. Try putting that in writing—*your goal in relation to material things and how you intend to reach it.* Example: "Because God is generous, I want to be generous. Specifically, I want to give away fifty percent of everything I grow this summer to an inner-city food bank."

5.   What do you think about the suggestion made in the session text about periodic review of your life choices? At what intervals do you feel you might make such as examination? Do you feel strongly enough to put it on the calendar?

6.   *To prepare for next session:* Write a brief summary of your personal work with this assignment. Then read the text for the next session.

SESSION 6

Food for the Journey

Several years ago we did some research on burnout among church leaders. "What are the conditions that lead to burnout?" we asked. Two answers emerged most frequently: "I've run out of inspiration" and "I feel alone."

Because of busyness, many of the people we surveyed had not taken time periodically to recharge their batteries. They attempted to live deeply committed lives in a state of chronic spiritual malnutrition. Further, although they had friends, they had no one with whom to share the high and low points of their work and prayer. They were hungry for community.

To live a life of compassion and justice as Jesus did is hard. It involves transforming individuals (beginning with ourselves) and institutions, recognizing and siding with the marginalized within and around us, bringing our ideals into everyday reality. Spiritual nourishment and companionship are essential if we are to be in this for the long haul. That is what this book has been about.

We have introduced several ways to nourish ourselves: commitment, listening, recalling our stories, cleansing, healing, and living with a generous spirit. Certain prayer forms have been offered: consecration, listening, intercession, confession, healing, and discernment. These have only scratched the surface. Other sources of spiritual power come to mind: play, meaningful work, sport, nature, expressive arts, friendship, gardening, doing nothing, ritual.

The ways to nourish our spirits are really endless. The question is, with limited time, which are right for me at this point in my life? This session focuses on the value of choosing food that nourishes particular hungers, finding community that is life-giving, and planning extended times for enrichment and refreshment.

✤ Choose Food That Nourishes Us ✤

During a retreat at Kirkridge in Bangor, Pennsylvania, Zalman Schachter and Eve Ilsen, trainers on the aging process, asked participants to "make up a menu for the rest of your lives." According to Kirkridge Director, Robert Raines, these questions were posed:

✤ What do I have appetite for?

✤ What do I want to taste again and again, or for the first time?

✤ What do I not want to stomach any longer?

✤ What, for me, would be a healthy diet for living?

Participants were encouraged not to censor their choices. Here are some that were mentioned:

"I want to sing more."

"I want a continuing sense of outrage about the injustices in our country."

"I want to ski more—the only time I feel graceful is when I'm skiing."

"I want quiet leisure to ponder Scripture or poetry and pray, coffee and the *New York Times* at hand."[1]

Schachter and Ilsen then invited those gathered to make up a menu for the rest of their lives. What an inviting idea!

We can use the same process to identify what we hunger for this present moment. What is it that we have appetite for now?

We posed this to a couple of friends. Without hesitation, one said, "I crave laziness. My work consumes too much of me." The other responded, "Everyone is telling me to lighten up. I want to play, but perhaps I've forgotten how."

Once our hunger is named, ways to satisfy it will surface. The one who craves laziness will take time to wander in the woods, watch clouds, or follow a whim. The woman who wants to play will start square dancing each Friday, or take an improvisational acting class that forces her to act ridiculous.

Is this too frivolous an approach to spiritual nourishment? We think not. It frees us to get out from under the "oughts" about what should be nourishing, and invites us to consider what really is. It places responsibility on us for deciding which particular hungers of body, mind, or spirit need attention. And it allows for flexibility in responding to changing needs. By tuning in to our present hunger, we eliminate practices that may have been effective in the past but are no longer helpful. Listening to our hunger when it cries for attention, we adjust our menu accordingly.

While such an approach is truly refreshing and provides variety, we have always combined it with core practices that we have found over time root us in God's grace. For us, this is a combination of some of the tools mentioned in this chapter: being consciously present to God, listening for guidance, meditation on readings written by those especially open to God. Consider making those practices that offer you stability and rootedness a core of your nourishment program.

Just as athletes have a physical fitness plan to keep them in top shape, you might benefit from creating a spiritual "fitness" plan. This could include both your core practice plus more spontaneous response to present hungers. If you do not find plans useful, commit to your own nourishment by reserving moments in your day to focus on opening yourself more consciously to God's presence in that moment.

Participate in Community

"If I want to jog every day, it helps if I hang around people who love to run," says a young friend of ours. That makes sense. To help us maintain a healthy way of life, it's good to have companions. The Christian life is not meant to be lived in isolation. To some of the early Christians, Paul wrote, "Weep with those who weep, rejoice with those who rejoice" (Rom. 12:15, NAB). To keep solidarity with one another in struggle and joy and to support our openness to God has always been the purpose of gathered communities of believers.

Jesus chose a small group to be with for company and for collaboration. The members supported one another in their struggle to grow. Successes and failures were reported to Jesus, who coached them into further growth.

Jesus believed in small numbers. Twelve were chosen as companions. Frequently, from among them, he selected two or three for special time apart. To take God's healing and forgiving work on the road, Jesus sent his disciples out in pairs. Gradually, faith communities were established to help members continue in the way the disciples had trod.

Four types of community have been sources of nourishment and support for us: small groups, established faith communities, spiritual guidance, and retreat.

Small Groups: Small groups have always been part of our lives. Rhoda now leads a centering prayer group weekly that meets first thing in the morning before work. Gathering around a candle, members sit in silence, desiring to be more receptive to the presence of God both there and in the day ahead. Our Partners gather regularly to witness and ritualize the unfolding of our lives—a seventieth birthday; a visit to our kindred community in Taizé, France; the birthing of a new vocation.

In addition to the importance of groups of several people, we have been struck by the efficacy of creative pairing. Two people committed to the same goal are a powerful small group. "Let's read a book together and discuss it," is the way some of our most productive endeavors have started. When members of our Partners Community taught together, we went out "two by two," Catholic paired with Protestant, and were tremendously enriched in the process.

Established Faith Communities: During all our adult lives, we have been members of local congregations. These have been conveyors of the faith traditions that have fed us so well. Not every congregation has continued to challenge and nourish us. At times it has seemed right to seek a new one. Fortunately, wherever we have lived, we have been able to find congregations that were right for that time.

A local parish is limited to one denominational perspective. To provide the breadth we long for, we have participated in activities and movements from other perspectives to provide the ecumenical approach that we consider so important.

We have tied into the larger faith community around the world by reading and praying the Scriptures designated by the ecumenical church for each Sunday worship. These readings follow the liturgical year, lifting up the great themes of advent, birth, penitence, death, rebirth, and empowerment.

Spiritual Guidance: At times, we have sought spiritual company more particularly tuned to our personal situation. Commonly called either spiritual direction or spiritual guidance, this art of companioning individuals in their relationship with God has come to the attention of a wider audience.

In the monastic tradition, certain members of the community were concerned with caring for the spiritual lives of the monks or nuns in their monastery. Now the tradition has expanded to include any person, male or female, lay or clergy, who feels called to do this work. Spiritual centers and seminaries offer training in the art of spiritual guidance.

The basic task of spiritual guidance is to help those guided tend their relationship with God. This affords them opportunity for regular encouragement, support, suggestions, and prayer with one who is committed to their growth.

Two forms of spiritual guidance have been fruitful in our lives. First, a relationship with a guide with whom we have no other connections. That provides an objectivity that is immensely valuable.[2] Second, we have operated informally as guides for one another, putting on "our spiritual guidance hat" when requested.[3]

Especially valuable in any of the forms of community mentioned are the elements of witness and accountability. To have someone witness our growth, a moment of confession, or a cause of celebration is immensely empowering. The church has always known this and provides rites and rituals for such moments as joining the community through baptism or covenanting with another in marriage. But many other moments are suitable for witness and celebration. These include starting a new work or finishing one, terminating a marriage, beginning a course of study or completing a degree, committing to a new step in growth, letting go of the children.

To keep you on track with whatever you decide to do related to nourishment, it is good to devise a system that works for you, perhaps involving another person or the community. For example, several neighbors agree to jog together each day. Or a group of people decide to garden together in a municipal plot, pooling their skill and experience.

Having a person or a community to report to, as the disciples did with Jesus, helps us see how God is moving in our lives. To do this for one another, that is, to give or receive a report of "the state of our union" with God is a profoundly loving act. Some people report verbally, others in writing or even with paints and clay, depicting the "shape of my life with God." To have another receive this, and then offer comments, strengthens our capacity to be more fully present to God in every dimension of our lives. A comment such as, "Your quiet time with God seems rich. What impact does this have on your work?" spurs us to greater depth.

Retreat: Most of us know the refreshment of getting away, leaving our regular routine at home and work. This describes retreat—a time away from daily preoccupations in order to refresh and rest our bodies, minds, and spirits. We have benefitted from two types of retreat—the content retreat through which we are exposed to new learnings or processes, and the silent retreat, in which we sink deeply into the presence of God without much exterior stimulation.

Content retreats are offered around the country at various centers. There we have learned to express ourselves through art and movement, to use writing as a tool for growth, to confront issues such as aging, homophobia, or environmental stewardship.

Silent retreats have been so beneficial for us that we participate in one every year. Reserving a favorite retreat center in advance and inviting an experienced leader to guide us, our Partners Community takes an overnight retreat in mid-September. This is a time to be still, allowing silence to descend gradually into our whole beings. Reducing outer and inner noise, we open ourselves to God's presence in the beauty of the retreat center, in our leader, and in ourselves. We have time, as Pope John XXIII said, "to read little but read well," to allow words and images to sink deep within. And we have space to discover our own images and learn their message. There we commune with God, ourselves, and nature, and mysteriously, even with our community, though we do not speak.

Spiritual nourishment does not happen automatically. It requires attention. All the practices and ways of prayer described in this book have one aim: to help us experience more fully the depth of God's love for us and to empower ourselves to share it more generously with others.

GROUP DESIGN

Purpose: To remember the nourishment we have experienced through this course, and to plan ways to continue growing in God's love.

A. Gathering Time, Large Group (*fifteen minutes*)

Focus on one life-style change you considered this week. Then share briefly. For example:

✤ "I've been recycling glass. Now I've added cans and plastic."

✤ "I decided to write on behalf of a political prisoner I learned about through Amnesty International."

✤ "At work we are unhappy about our expected move. I've decided to bring something humorous and share it each day with my colleagues."

B. Check-in Time on the Reading, Large Group (*fifteen minutes*)

Share freely and briefly on:
1.   Which points in the chapter resonated with you and why?
2.   Which suggestions made in the chapter would you like to explore further?

C. Remembering the Nourishment We've Experienced (*twenty-five minutes*)

1. *Large Group:* Someone read aloud the summary outline of this course in the introduction. Then review your own notes. Identify one or two ways you felt nourished during the course.
2. *Pairs:* Share the ways you've been nourished.
3. *Large Group:*

    a. Spontaneously share what you just spoke about in pairs regarding what has nourished you.

    b. As closure for what you have experienced together, consider completing these sentences or choose something more appropriate:

      ✚ "I'm grateful for . . ."

      ✚ "I learned . . ."

      ✚ "I feel disappointed . . ."

      ✚ "I hope . . ."

D. Food for the Journey (*ten minutes*)

1. *Large Group:* Someone read aloud the Kirkridge questions on page 77.
2. *Ones:* Jot down your answers.
3. *Large Group:* Share some of your answers to encourage and stimulate one another.

E. Going Deeper (*forty minutes*)

1. *Ones:* Reflect on various areas of your life, keeping the Kirkridge questions in mind:

✛ work

✛ church

✛ home

✛ global concerns

✛ community

✛ other

2. Jot down your responses.

3. Looking at these responses and your first reactions choose one or two items that would form a healthy diet for your living now. Call this your spiritual fitness plan. Write on a clean sheet of paper.

4. *Fours:* For accountability and witnessing, share your plans. Give each other feedback, encouragement. Ask for any help you might need in living your plan.

E. Closing, Large Group (*twenty minutes*)

1. Place spiritual fitness plans in middle of circle on the floor.

2. Stand together, arms around each other. In a way appropriate to your group, receive God's blessing on you as you commit to live more deeply in God's love.

3. Devise a way to celebrate the completion of the course, using music, movement, prayer, refreshments, or other ways you create.

INDIVIDUAL WORK

(For people who are working by themselves with the course material)

Purpose: to reflect on the practices you have found important in this course and to plan ways to continue growing in God's love.

1. *Integration:* Reread the Kirkridge questions referred to in Section D of the Group Design. Then write your answers to the four questions. Take time to do this prayerfully. You may want to ask God's guidance, especially as you consider what kind of help you need now.

2. Devise a way to symbolize what this course has meant for you. You may want to do this alone or with another person. Ritualizing our current experience of healing, renewal, questioning, and dedication can give us a greater sense of our own inner realities and a deeper respect for our own spiritual journey. You might incorporate appropriate readings and song, and use candles, nature objects, or personal objects important to you.

NEXT STEPS

In the midst of strife among peoples and escalating damage to the environment, we are called to be people of hope, to carry within ourselves a picture of creation as God envisioned it to be. The mystic Howard Thurman described this in colorful language, "a friendly world of friendly folk beneath a friendly sky."[1]

This is God's dream. And if we are people of God, it is our dream as well, not simply to hold, but to bring into being.

This means that in the midst of a labor dispute, a medical emergency, an 8 A.M. traffic jam, or a rush order for our product, we are invited to have a drink of "living water," to eat the bread that satisfies, to plant ourselves in the fertile soil of God. Thus nourished by God's love, we are to be open channels for that love to flow to others.

In *Journeying with the Spirit*, we have learned ways to nurture the presence of love deep within. Challenging questions have been examined:

✤ how to respond wholeheartedly to God's invitation to be loved and to love;

✤ how to cultivate the art of listening deeply to God, ourselves, and others;

✤ how to interpret what my journey is saying about God's generosity and love;

✤ how to be a healed and healing person in a world of hurt;

✤ how to make life choices that express the peace, wholeness, generosity, and compassion of Jesus;

✤ how to arrange for nourishment that truly satisfies as I move through my life.

This is a tall order, but not impossible. We are part of what David and Barbara Sorensen call "a magnificent conspiracy with world-wide implications" of people who believe that when we "begin to embrace the gospel—not just believe it but live it out—people get fed, children find homes, and families find peace."[2] As part of this conspiracy, we are in good company.

Our next step might be to practice the tools learned in this book. Most of them do require repetition in order to become a natural part of our lives. In fact, according to the Sorensens, it takes six weeks to establish a new habit. As we select which tools we want to incorporate into our lives, we can devise a system for doing that.

We also could look at the same tools from a social viewpoint, asking ourselves, for example, in what ways we could listen more broadly to people different from us. Or in what ways do we cooperate with unjust social systems and thus need conversion from that.

Another possibility is to find and use tools more particularly geared to our situation and to the future for which we want to work. For example, to nurture the interconnections of world peoples and systems, we might commit to living creatively with diversity, being open to friendships with people unlike ourselves. To learn to grow from conflict, we might study conflict-management tools. To understand people of other faiths, we might decide to root ourselves firmly in our own tradition while opening ourselves to other' traditions.

Another step would be to consider working with one of the other books in the *Doorways* Series. To ground our growth in the reality of God as discovered by the Hebrew people, we could turn to *Encountering God in the Old Testament*. For focused exposure to the love of Jesus, consider *Meeting Jesus in the New Testament*. To discern our focus for action, we might explore *Discovering Your Gifts, Vision, and Call*.

Whatever our next step, it is fitting at the end of this book to consider the connection between hope and prayer as described by New Testament scholar Walter Wink:

> Hope envisions its future and then acts as if that future is irresistible, thus helping to create the reality for which it longs. The future is not closed, though there are forces whose interactions are somewhat predictable. But how they will interact is not.
>
> Even a small number of people, totally committed to the new inevitability on which they have fixed their imaginations, can decisively affect the shape the future takes. These shapers of the future are the intercessors who call out of the future the longed-for new present; they believe the future into being. In the New Testament, the name and texture and aura of that future is the reign of God.[3]

Whether that future is a better relationship with a colleague on the job or a sustaining environment for all the children of the world, it is exhilarating to know that we are called and nourished by God to believe it into being.

ADDITIONAL RESOURCES

For more on commitment:

Anderson, Sherry Ruth, and Hopkins, Patricia. *The Feminine Face of God: The Unfolding of the Sacred in Women.* New York, Bantam Books, 1991. Interviews with women on how they have discovered and lived their spiritual commitment.

Gibbard, Mark. *Twelve Who Prayed, Twentieth Century Models of Prayer.* Minneapolis: Augsburg Publishing, 1977. Examples of commitment to the life of prayer and service.

O'Connor, Elizabeth. *Call to Commitment.* New York: Harper & Row, 1963. The story of the commitment lived by those associated with the Church of the Saviour, Washington, D.C.

Smith, Hannah Whitall. *The Christian's Secret of a Happy Life.* New York: Ballantine/Epiphany, division of Random House, 1991. A classic on how to live the life of faith.

Listening to God, self, and others:

Berne, Patricia H., and Savary, Louis M. *Dream Symbol Work, Unlocking the Energy from Dreams and Spiritual Experiences.* Mahwah, NJ: Paulist Press, 1991. Ways to uncover the message that dreams carry.

Bracey, Hyler; Rosenblum, Jack; Sanford, Aubrey; and Trueblood, Roy. *Managing from the Heart.* New York: Delacorte Press, 1990. The human side of management where people give importance to listening well to one another.

Hart, Thomas N. *The Art of Christian Listening.* Mahwah, NJ: Paulist Press, 1980. The many ways in which we can serve others through listening to their stories. Gives special attention to counseling and spiritual direction.

Tannen, Deborah, Ph.D. *You Just Don't Understand: Women and Men in Conversation*. New York: Ballantine Books, 1990. A specialist in linguistics helps us understand each other by shedding light on deeply rooted differences in our ways of communicating.

Thich Nhat Hanh. *The Miracle of Mindfulness: A Manual on Meditation*. Boston: Beacon Press, 1987. Practical exercises for both beginners and people familiar with meditation for greater self-understanding and peacefulness.

On Life Stories:

Boulding, Elise. *Born Remembering*. Pendle Hill Pamphlet, March 1975. A beautifully written spiritual autobiography of a woman who searched until she found spiritual nourishment.

Fowler, Jim, and Keen, Sam. *Life Maps: Conversations on the Journey of Faith*. Waco, TX: Word Books, 1980. Conversation between two creative thinkers about faith and how it develops.

Jung, Carl G. *Memories, Dreams, Reflections*. New York: Random House, 1965. The autobiography of a great twentieth-century figure in psychology and the story of his search for the key to the unconscious life.

Raines, Robert A. *Going Home: A Personal Story of Self-Discovery, a Journey from Despair to Hope*. New York: Crossroad Publishing, 1985. A clergyman's account of how he had to let go of basic certainties before something new could be born.

Healing of mind and spirit:

Houston, Jean. *The Search for the Beloved, Journeys in Mythology and Sacred Psychology*. Los Angeles: J. P. Tarcher, 1987.

MacNutt, Francis. *Healing*. Notre Dame, IN: Ave Maria Press, 1974. A down-to-earth treatment of the ministry of healing in the Christian context. Combines practical experience with psychological insights and deep faith.

May, Gerald G., M.D. *Addiction and Grace*. San Francisco: Harper & Row, 1988. Explores the psychology of addiction, its relationship to the spiritual life, and the role of human freedom and grace in our journey to health.

May, Gerald G., M.D. *Care of Mind—Care of Spirit*. San Francisco: Harper & Row, 1982. May, a psychiatrist and spiritual director, writes with insight and experience about inner growth. Especially helpful for those who counsel others on the religious quest.

Life Choices:

Fox, Matthew. *Creation Spirituality, Liberating Gifts for the People of the Earth*. San Francisco: HarperSanFrancisco, 1991. Discuss the influence of social justice, feminism, and environmentalism on life choices.

Gore, Senator Al. *Earth in the Balance: Ecology and the Human Spirit*. New York: Houghton Mifflin, 1992. Analyzes the causes of our environmental crisis and offers a comprehensive plan of action with personal and social dimensions.

Haughey, John C., S.J. *The Holy Use of Money: Personal Finances in Light of Christian Faith*. Garden City, NY: Doubleday, 1986. How to reconcile the material and religious spheres of our lives. Economic decisions made from a faith perspective.

Ryan, Thomas. *Wellness, Spirituality and Sports*. Mahwah, NJ: Paulist Press, 1987. Shows connection between physical and spiritual fitness. Special emphasis on nourishing aspects of running, swimming, skiing, and dancing.

Church as a source of spiritual growth:
   Dozier, Verna J. *The Dream of God: A Call to Return*. Boston:
   Cowley Publications, 1991. Calls the laity to a revision-
   ing and reshaping of church.

To continue the growth process offered in the *Doorways* Series,
consider:
   Encountering God in the Old Testament. To examine the question "Who is God?" and to experience God as creator,
   caller, deliverer, Covenant-Maker, suffering servant, and
   new song. This offers a foundation for understanding our
   spiritual roots.
   Meeting Jesus in the New Testament. To understand how Jesus
   related to God and to see how he can ground us more
   deeply in God's love and justice.
   Discovering Your Gifts, Vision, and Call. To continue explo-
   ration of call and to relate that with God's vision and our
   gifts.

   The *Doorways* Series, when offered in a parish, can be a cata-
lyst for change in individuals and in the congregation. To learn
more about how a parish can foster the spiritual journeys of members plus organize to support each one's vision, call, and gifts, in-
quire about the authors' "Recreating the Church" packet of articles:
1309 Merchant Lane, McLean, VA 22101.

   As a follow-up to this course, some people have found value
in reading the Scriptures selected for the coming Sunday liturgy.
Typically these include a selection from the Hebrew Scriptures,
the Psalms, the Epistles, and the Gospels. Many churches follow
an ecumenical lectionary shared by Roman Catholic and a number of Protestant denominations. By meditating on these readings,
based on the rhythm of the liturgical year, one joins the many
churches around the world using them.

Retreat and workshop opportunities:

Dayspring Retreat Center, 11301 Neelsville Church Road, Germantown, MD 20876. Phone: (301) 428-9348. A place of silence and solitude providing meditative retreats for individuals and groups.

Faith at Work, 150 So. Washington St., #204, Falls Church, VA 22046. Phone: (703) 237-3426. A national network of people at the growing edge of the church who are committed to biblical faith and new models of ministry. Offers conferences and publications.

Friends of Creation Spirituality, 134 Coleen St., Livermore, CA 94550. Phone: (510) 449-1261. Offers workshops based in creation spirituality. Includes body prayer, seminars, art as meditation, and celebration.

Kirkridge, Bangor, PA 18013. Phone: (215) 588-1793. Offers retreats and workshops on a variety of themes.

Wellspring, 11411 Neelsville Church Road, Germantown, MD 20874. Phone: (301) 428-3373. Offers events to help people dream about and experience new structures for church communities.

Wernersville Retreat Center, Jesuit Center for Spiritual Growth, Wernersville, PA 19565. Phone: (215) 678-8085. Offers directed retreats of varying lengths. Includes time alone with Scripture plus a daily conference with a retreat guide/director.

ACKNOWLEDGMENTS

Like all books, this one has a story behind it. Telling that story allows us to thank all the people who helped along the way and also gives you, the reader, some background on how this was written and why.

In a sense this book began when Lois Donnelly, a Catholic, joined with Jackie McMakin and Pat Davis, both Protestants, to offer workshops and courses in local churches. Jean Sweeney and Rhoda Nary, both Catholics, soon joined us. We took the name Partners because we experienced great creativity when as Catholics and Protestants we partnered together to do our work.

Some of us received training in experiential design from Faith at Work. We were inspired by the work of the Taizé Community in France, started by Roger Schutz, a Swiss Reformed pastor, who drew together Roman Catholic and Protestant men to live a monastic life dedicated to "a passion for unity."

Becoming dissatisfied with our "piecemeal" workshops and courses, we were ready for what became a life-changing question: "If you could do anything you wanted in churches, what would it be?"

We had been students at the Church of the Saviour's School of Christian Living and had been deeply affected by the courses offered there. Founded by Gordon and Mary Cosby, its story has been chronicled by Elizabeth O'Connor. Could we design a similar set of courses that would present the treasures of both Catholic and Protestant traditions in a format that busy people could respond to?

What resulted were the four courses contained in the *Doorways* Series. When they were offered, several participants wanted to join us in the Partners Community: Susan Hogan, Cathie Bates, Dave Scheele, Mid Allen, Ricci Waters, Sally Dowling, Sancy Scheele, Coby Pieterman, and Charlotte Rogers. Each of these people added their ideas to the courses as we developed them further.

Participants then began to ask, "Could you give us the course materials so we could facilitate them ourselves and take them to other places?"

Jackie began to translate the notes and outlines into book form but soon got bogged down. Rhoda volunteered to help, and from then on we worked together, Jackie as writer, Rhoda as editor, both as conceptualizers. The Partners gave tremendous support throughout the process and helped a great deal with finishing touches. Others who helped were Mim Dinndorf, Sonya Dyer, Mary Elizabeth Hunt, Maggie Kalil, Gertrude Kramer, Billie Johansen, Mary Pockman, Janet Rife, Mary Scantlebury, and Gretchen Hannon. Our first editor was Cy Riley from Winston Press.

Liberation, black, creation, and feminist theologies have shown us how limited are our contemporary thought patterns and organizational structures. These theologies stress the Gospel's "preferential option for the poor," the importance of valuing and incorporating the experience of nonwhite, Third World, female, oppressed, and marginalized persons.

In such a theologically fertile period, when new understandings are being lived, shared, and written about at an amazing rate, each choice of word, phrase, or emphasis has theological implications. Whatever we write, in one sense, is quickly dated. Yet, in another sense, we are trying to capture and describe some of the timeless aspects of Christian faith. This book would serve a good purpose if our attempts to preserve the old and incorporate the new stimulated each of you to do this personally.

Since first published in 1984, the *Doorways* Series has found its way to several countries outside our own, most notably Mexico. There it has enjoyed wide use. A Spanish translation called *Puertas al Encuentro*, including Mexican examples, was created by Mari Carmen Mariscal and associates.[1] Several stories of our Mexican friends are included in this revision.

For this new edition, we are indebted to editor Kandace Hawkinson for seeing the possibility of a brand-new format—each course presented in a single book. She and her fellow editor, Ron Klug, have been wonderful to work with. Others here at home have been a big help, some for the second time: Millie Adams, Marjorie Bankson, Connie Francis, Lynn Pareut, Ellen Radday, Gay Bland, Gretchen Hannon, Martha Hlavin, Mary Moore, and Valerie Vesser. Our husbands, Dave McMakin and Bill Nary, and our children, Tom and Peg McMakin and Brendan, Kristin, Kevin, and Paul Nary, have given lots of support, each in different ways.

We would like to hear from you about any reactions and suggestions you have that will help improve this approach to strengthening your spiritual life. If you would like us to partner with you as you consider next steps after using the *Doorways* Series, we are available for consultation, training, and retreats.

Jacqueline McMakin
1309 Merchant Lane
McLean, VA 22101
(703) 827-0336

Rhoda Nary
4820 N. 27th Place
Arlington, VA 22207
(703) 538-6132

NOTES

Introduction

1. William Callahan, *Noisy Contemplations* (Mt. Ranier, MD: Quixote Center, 1982), p. 24.

2. Callahan, *Noisy Contemplations*, p. 7.

Session 1

1. Pierre Teilhard de Chardin, *The Divine Milieu* (New York: Harper & Row, 1960), p. 105.

2. Teilhard de Chardin, *Divine Milieu*, p. 31.

3. Teilhard de Chardin, *Divine Milieu*, p. 62.

4. Dorothee Sölle, *Choosing Life* (Philadelphia: Fortress Press, 1981), p. 19.

5. Gerald G. May, *The Awakened Heart* (San Francisco: HarperSanFrancisco, 1991), p. 65.

6. May, *Awakened Heart*, pp. 65–66.

7. Thomas Merton, *The Sign of Jonas* (New York: Harcourt, Brace, 1953), p. 76.

8. Merton, *Sign of Jonas*, p. 76.

9. Merton, *Sign of Jonas*, p. 76.

10. Sherry Ruth Anderson and Patricia Hopkins, *The Feminine Face of God: The Unfolding of the Sacred in Women* (New York: Bantam Books, 1991), p. 10.

11. Anderson and Hopkins, *Feminine Face of God*, p. 10.

12. Anderson and Hopkins, *Feminine Face of God*, p. 18.

13. Anderson and Hopkins, *Feminine Face of God*, p. 48.

14. Anderson and Hopkins, *Feminine Face of God*, p. 69.

15. In *Discovering Your Gifts, Vision, and Call*, we deal in greater detail with the question of woundedness leading to larger reality.

Session 2

1. Dody Donnelly, *Team* (Mahwah, NJ: Paulist Press, 1977), p. 78.

2. Carl G. Jung, *Memories, Dreams, Reflections* (New York: Random House, 1965), p. 170.

3. *At a Journal Workshop* (New York: Dialogue House Library, 1975). This book describes Ira Progoff's basic process.

4. Thomas N. Hart, *The Art of Christian Listening* (Mahwah, NJ: Paulist Press, 1980), p. 18.

5. Don McDermott, "Listening with My Heart," *Faith at Work*, March/April 1991, p. 13.

6. McDermott, "Listening with My Heart," p. 13.

7. Thomas Kelly, *A Testament of Devotion* (New York: Harper & Brothers, 1941), p. 29.

Session 3

1. Mark Gibbard, *Twelve Who Prayed, Twentieth Century Models of Prayer* (Minneapolis: Augsburg Publishing, 1977), p. 21.

2. Jean Haldane, paraphrase from "A Study of the Laity," *Action Information*, June 1975, pp. 1–4. Out of this study and the subsequent discussions of it in the host church, Jean Haldane came up with these questions churches could ask themselves:

   • Should not a goal of church life be to help people articulate and share their spiritual journeys?

   • When this happens and people become aware of next steps to take, can the church be available to assist these steps?

   • Should not every church have ways to encourage this companioning of people on their pilgrimages and perhaps train people to facilitate this?

3. Another way to represent your life is to make a photographic collage. Collect photos that represent various facets of your life. Photocopy each picture. To heighten the artistry of this project, cut around figures and shapes. Then, on a fairly large (18-x-18 inches) piece of artist's paper, arrange your photos in a way that conveys meaning to you. Fasten each with rubber cement. This is fascinating to do in a group. Thanks to Jean Adams, who led us through this activity.

4. Sherry Ruth Anderson and Patricia Hopkins, *The Feminine Face of God: The Unfolding of the Sacred in Women* (New York: Bantam Books, 1991), p. 58.

5. Jung, *Memories, Dreams, Reflections*, pp. 45–46.

6. Anderson and Hopkins, *Feminine Face of God*, p. 35.

7. Elise Boulding, *Born Remembering*, Pendle Hill Pamphlet, March 1975, p. 6.

8. Marilyn Ferguson, *The Aquarian Conspiracy* (Los Angeles: J. P. Tarcher, 1980), p. 344.

9. Boulding, *Born Remembering*, p. 16.

10. Boulding, *Born Remembering*, p. 16.

11. Boulding, *Born Remembering*, p. 16.

12. Robert A. Raines, *Going Home* (New York: Crossroad Publishing, 1985), p. 16.

13. Raines, *Going Home*, p. 16.

14. Raines, *Going Home*, p. 123.

15. Robert McAfee Brown, *Creative Dislocation: The Movement of Grace* (Nashville: Abingdon, 1980), p. 144.

Session 4

1. Ruth Carter Stapleton, *The Gift of Inner Healing* (Waco, TX: Word Books, 1976); Francis MacNutt, *Healing* (Notre Dame, IN: Ave Maria Press, 1974); Dennis Linn and Matthew Linn, *Healing of Memories* (New York: Paulist Press, 1974); Dennis Linn and Matthew Linn, *Healing Life's Hurts* (New York: Paulist Press, 1978).

2. T. Ralph Morton, *What Is the Iona Community?* (Glasgow: Iona Community Publishing Department, 1957). Obtainable from Community House, 214 Clyde Street, Glasgow G 1 4JZ, Scotland. The Iona Community, *Divine Healing* (Glasgow: Iona Community Publishing Department, no date given). Obtainable from Community House.

3. Materials available from the Christian Fellowship of Healing, c/o Morningside Congregational Church, 15 Chamberlain Road, Edinburgh EH 10 4DJ, Scotland.

4. Dietrich Bonhoeffer, *Life Together* (New York: Harper & Row, 1954), pp. 112–13.

5. Agnes Sanford, *Sealed Orders* (Plainfield, NJ: Logos International, 1972). This is the story of Agnes Sanford's work in healing. The process for healing of memories is described more fully by Agnes Sanford in *The Healing Gifts of the Spirit* (San Francisco: Harper & Row, 1984), pp. 125–41.

Session 5

1. Thomas Kelly, "The Eternal Now and Social Concern," in *A Testament of Devotion* (New York: Harper & Row, 1941).

2. Kelly, "The Eternal Now," pp. 106–7.

3. Kelly, "The Eternal Now," p. 109.

4. Barbara DeGrote-Sorensen and David Allen Sorensen, *'Tis a Gift to Be Simple* (Minneapolis: Augsburg Fortress, 1992), p. 8.

5. DeGrote-Sorensen and Sorensen, *'Tis a Gift*, p. 8.

6. DeGrote-Sorensen and Sorensen, *'Tis a Gift*, p. 8.

7. In Lester R. Brown, *State of the World 1991* (New York: W. W. Norton, 1991), p. 165.

8. Brown, *State of the World*, p. 169.

9. Parker Palmer, *The Active Life: A Spirituality of Work, Creativity, and Caring* (San Francisco: Harper & Row, 1990). Palmer devotes a chapter to a discussion on scarcity and abundance. Killian Noe, in a sermon preached on May 10, 1992, at the Church of the Saviour, built on Palmer's analysis. We are indebted to both of these thinkers for our summary of this perspective.

10. Malvina Reynolds, copyright 1955, 1958 by Northern Music Co., 445 Park Avenue, New York, NY 10022.

11. See Thomas A. Green, S.J., *Weeds Among the Wheat: Discernment Where Prayer and Action Meet* (Notre Dame, IN: Ave Maria Press, 1984).

12. DeGrote-Sorensen and Sorensen, *'Tis a Gift*, p. 16.

13. This summarizes some of Esther de Waal's interpretation of Benedictine vows in *Seeing God: The Way of St. Benedict* (Collegeville, MN: The Liturgical Press, 1984).

14. Quoted by Kay Schultz in "Hope in the City," *Faith at Work*, March/April 1992, p. 9.

Session 6

1. Robert Raines, in *The Ridgeleaf* (Newsletter from Kirkridge, Bangor, PA 18013), no. 190, May 1992.

2. Some useful descriptions of this form of spiritual direction are Tilden Edwards, *Spiritual Friend* (New York: Paulist Press, 1980); Kenneth Leech, *Soul Friend* (San Francisco: HarperSanFrancisco, 1992); Thomas Merton, *Spiritual Direction and Meditation* (Collegeville, MN: Liturgical Press, 1960).

3. A helpful resource for offering mutual spiritual direction is Dorothy Devers, *Faithful Friendship* (Cincinnati: Forward Movement Publications, 1980), 412 Sycamore Street, Cincinnati, OH 45202.

Next Steps

1. As quoted by Verna J. Dozier, *The Dream of God: A Call to Return* (Boston: Cowley Publications, 1991), p. 31.

2. DeGrote-Sorensen and Sorensen, *'Tis a Gift*, p. 93.

3. "History Belongs to the Intercessors: Co-Creating with God Through Prayer," *Sojourners*, October 1990.

Acknowledgments

1. Available from Edamex, Heriberto Frias #1104, Mexico 03100, D. F. Mexico, or from the authors.